TRILBY JAMES

Trilby James read Drama at Bristol University before completing the three-year acting course at RADA. She graduated in 1990 and over the years has worked extensively as an actor in theatre, film and television. In 2000 she also began working as a freelance director and teacher at several leading drama schools including ALRA, Arts Educational Schools, Royal Central School of Speech and Drama, East 15, Mountview Academy of Theatre Arts and the Royal Academy of Dramatic Art where she is now an Associate Teacher. She continues to work across courses, directing third-year performances as well as teaching first and second-year students and running workshops for shorter programmes. She is a script reader and dramaturg for Kali Theatre Company and has directed several play-readings for their 'Talkback' seasons.

THE GOOD AUDITION GUIDES

CLASSICAL MONOLOGUES
edited by Marina Caldarone

CONTEMPORARY MONOLOGUES
edited by Trilby James

SHAKESPEARE MONOLOGUES
edited by Luke Dixon

SHAKESPEARE MONOLOGUES FOR YOUNG PEOPLE
edited by Luke Dixon

The Good Audition Guides

CONTEMPORARY MONOLOGUES FOR WOMEN

edited and introduced by

TRILBY JAMES

NICK HERN BOOKS
London
www.nickhernbooks.co.uk

A NICK HERN BOOK

The Good Audition Guides:
Contemporary Monologues for Women
first published in Great Britain in 2014
by Nick Hern Books Limited
The Glasshouse, 49a Goldhawk Road, London W12 8QP

Introduction copyright © 2014 Trilby James
Copyright in this selection © 2014 Nick Hern Books Ltd

Designed and typeset by Nick Hern Books, London
Printed and bound by CPI Group (UK) Ltd

A CIP catalogue record for this book
is available from the British Library

ISBN 978 1 85459 564 5

Contents

6

8

Introduction

☞ WHY CONTEMPORARY?

Whether you are still at school auditioning for a youth theatre, about to leave school and want to go to drama school, at drama school looking for showcase material, or a young professional actor preparing for a specific audition, a well-chosen contemporary monologue will be a key component in your audition repertoire. It should reflect something of your own taste and, depending on the style of writing, may provide an opportunity to show something more intimate, more televisual than a classical speech might allow.

The fifty monologues in this volume are from plays that have been written post-2000. With the odd exception the characters range in age from fourteen to thirty-five. There is a wide variety of character types and styles of writing from which to choose. They are all drawn from the extensive list of new plays published by Nick Hern Books.

☞ CHOOSING YOUR MONOLOGUE

I have often likened finding the perfect monologue to finding the perfect pair of jeans. It is rarely a case of 'one size fits all'. You might have to try on several pairs, in different stores, before you find the cut that works for you, but once you have, you will feel confident in the knowledge that you are looking and feeling your best. So it is with audition speeches. You need to find pieces that suit you, that you cannot wait to perform and that will get even better with wear.

If you are auditioning for a youth theatre:

- You will be judged on your potential and your willingness to be open, honest and free. Nobody is looking for a polished or over-rehearsed performance. It is best therefore to choose pieces that allow you to express yourself and for a panel to see something of who you really are.

- Choose something close to you in age and type. Something to which you can relate. Something that inspires you, from a play that speaks to you.

- Avoid accents unless you are really good at them.

If you are auditioning for drama school:

- And have been asked to prepare a classical speech, choose a contemporary monologue that will provide contrast. For example, you may have a Shakespearean monologue that is pensive or tragic so opt for something comic. Similarly, if your classical speech is light in tone, choose something that shows off a more serious side.

If you are already at drama school:

- And you are looking to extend your range, you will want to choose a monologue that stretches you. Perhaps you are studying a particular accent or type of character quite different from yourself.

- And are looking for showcase material, think about how you wish to present yourself. Consider whether you are right for the part you have chosen and whether, if there was to be another production of the play, you could be easily cast in the role.

If you are auditioning for a specific role in a professional production (and have been asked to prepare an additional piece that is not from the play for which you are being seen):

- Choose something close to the part for which you are auditioning.

- Consider the language of the piece and whether you are after something heightened and obviously theatrical or whether you require something more intimate, and realistic.

If you are looking to extend your showreel:

- It may sound obvious, but think about what sort of speeches would be best suited to the varying demands of radio or television.

☞ PREPARING YOUR MONOLOGUE

- Learn your speeches well in advance of the actual audition. Should you forget your lines the panel will be able to tell whether it is out of nervousness or insufficient preparation.

- Read the play. You may be asked questions about it or be required to improvise around it.

- Undertake all necessary research. Make a study of the historical, social and political world of the play. Be sure to understand the meaning of unfamiliar words and references. If the character's accent is not native to you, work hard to perfect it.

- Remain flexible in the way you perform/stage your monologue. Be prepared to be redirected in an audition.

- Using props. There are no hard-and-fast rules about the use of stage properties at an audition. However, common sense suggests that, if you can easily carry an object in your pocket (i.e. a letter, a ring, a handkerchief, etc.), by all means bring this to an audition. If the object to which you refer is large, imagine it is there, or, if necessary, mime using it. Some might even argue that miming props is simpler, and in certain cases much more practical. In any event, you need not worry about being 'marked down' by your decision either to use real objects or to mime using them. What is important is that they do not become burdensome and get in the way of your acting.

- Try not to get stuck in a mode of delivery. It is useful to consider that, unless a character is making a political or after-dinner speech, chances are they have no idea they are going to speak for such a long time. They may make a statement, perhaps as a response to a specific question; then having made that statement they might need to qualify it. They might then be reminded of something else they wish to add and so on. In this way, a monologue can be regarded as a series of interrelated thoughts. Communicating a character's thought processes is fundamental to any acting technique. In the case of an audition, it takes the pressure off having to deliver a load of text. It allows you to stay fresh, to be in the moment and to make spontaneous choices. Before you start, all you need worry about is the trigger – the reason for saying what you do. Then have the courage to take it thought by thought and allow yourself to be surprised. In this way the monologue should feel slightly different every time.

- It is vital that you use your imagination to envisage all that the character sees and describes. If you are still seeing the page on which the speech is written, you know you are doing something wrong. Provide images for yourself so that in your mind's eye you quite literally lift the speech from the page.

- Timing/editing. Most speeches at audition should last no longer than two minutes. Some of the monologues in this edition are slightly longer, some shorter. Some I have cut, and some I have edited from a duologue with another character, and some have been augmented by joining two or more passages which appear separately in the original text. I have inserted this empty bracket symbol [...] to show where a cut has been made. Once you have read the whole play, you may have ideas of your own about what and what not to include.

☞ THE AUDITION

You will find there are many useful books on the market that make a complete study of this subject, from what to wear to how to enter and exit a room. These are some of the basics:

- *Manage your nerves.* Try to put the increased adrenaline you are experiencing to good use. Approach the audition with a positive sense of excitement, something to which you have been looking forward as opposed to something you have been dreading. Nervous energy, if correctly channelled, can help at an audition. Conversely you should avoid being under-energised. If you are someone who reacts lethargically to increased stress, you may need to do a good warm-up before you arrive.

- *Take ownership of the situation.* Before you begin, take a moment to imagine the space you are in as the location of the monologue. The best auditions are those in which the actor successfully transports the panel from, say, 'Studio One or Two' (or whatever the room you are auditioning in is called) to an urban street, a clearing in the woods, a room in a flat in modern Russia, etc. Take time to think about where you will place the other character/s in the scene and, before you speak, allow yourself a moment to hear what has been said to you or to imagine what has just happened that prompts you to say the things you do. Do not rush the speech. Take your time. In the case of a drama–school audition, remember that you will be paying for this privilege!

* *Empower yourself.* There is no good reason why the panel should want you to fail. If you are auditioning for a youth group or a drama school, consider that the panel are willing you to do well, even if they are not necessarily giving that impression. If you have been asked to be seen for a specific role, it is because the director is serious about you for the job. It is possible that the panel are equally anxious about the impression they may give you. Remember, you only have control over your part of the audition process. There is no point speculating, worrying about whether they will want you in their group, school or offer you the part. Just take care of your side of things, and be safe in the knowledge that, whatever happens, you tried your best.

☞ HOW TO USE THIS BOOK

For each monologue, I have provided a list of the following:

☞ WHO   The character's name, their age, and where they come from. As a general rule, it is best to avoid accents unless they are native to you, or you have a good ear for them, or you wish to practise them. If the character's accent is not native to you, you may like to try playing the speech in your own accent, but watch out for speeches that have been written with a strong dialect or idiom. These do not translate well as they disturb the rhythm and overall feeling of the piece.

☞ TO WHOM   It is useful to think of a monologue as an uninterrupted duologue or dialogue. Rather than talking to a blank wall, see if you can visualise the person or people to whom you are speaking. Cast them in your mind's eye. Imagine their reactions as you progress with your speech. How does their response in turn affect you. Are you in love with them? Do they make you blush? Do you feel negatively towards them? Can you read their disapproval? Whatever the relationship, the panel will need to believe that you are actually talking to somebody. It is advisable, by the way, not to look directly at the panel, unless they ask you to do so.

Direct audience address: If your character is talking to the audience, make a decision about who the audience are to you. Are they your friend and your confidante? Are they more like an analyst with whom you feel safe to reveal your innermost thoughts? Are they a sort of sounding board? Are they judging you? Do you need to explain yourself or to convince them in some way? It is still advisable not to look at the actual panel in this case, but imagine an audience just above their heads and direct your speech there.

☞ WHERE   For the most part, this is specified in the text. Take a moment before you start your speech to imagine the location.

☞ WHEN   Most of the monologues in this volume are set in the present day. Some are historical. Read the play to make further decisions about the time of year, day of the week and the time of day it is.

☞ WHAT TO CONSIDER   This will include the style of the play, its themes and use of language, the character's backstory and some indication about what happens next.

☞ WHAT SHE WANTS   Objectives to play. Once you have learned your speech, done all the necessary research and provided images for yourself of all that your character describes, the only thing you should be actively playing is the 'What do I want?' or the 'What do I have to have?'

☞ KEYWORDS   There are usually one or two keywords in a sentence that portray the meaning. This does not mean to say that you should overemphasise these words or use increased volume, rather be aware that they are often specifically chosen by the character for a purpose or resonate in a way that may be out of the ordinary. You will probably find that these are the words to which you will need to connect (intellectually and imaginatively) in order to get beneath the skin of your character. In some cases, the writer is so descriptive that you will be able to add more words to the list as it stands.

*

These prompts are a suggestion only. When you become increasingly familiar with your speech, you will find you have opinions of your own; you may even find yourself in disagreement. No two actors are exactly alike just as no two people can be. It is a very personal endeavour. Use this book as a starting point from which you will form your own ideas. It is by no means a substitute for reading the play, but rather a tool intended to help, to provoke and hopefully to inspire.

The Monologues

Airsick

Emma Frost

☞ **WHO**   Scarlet, early thirties, from London.

☞ **TO WHOM**   The audience (see note on 'Direct audience address' in the introduction).

☞ **WHERE**   Her friend Lucy's flat in East London. The scene starts in Lucy's living/dining room. Then, as the lights go down, Scarlet moves towards the audience to deliver her speech.

☞ **WHEN**   Summer 2002.

☞ **WHAT HAS JUST HAPPENED**   Lucy, recently returned from New York, has made supper for her American boyfriend Joe (also newly arrived from New York), her father Mick, her best friend Scarlet and Gabriel, a New Zealander whom Lucy met at the airport (on her return from New York and in advance of Joe), and who is now lodging with Mick. As the lights go down on the scene, Scarlet moves towards us.

☞ **WHAT TO CONSIDER**

- The speech comes randomly and is not altogether connected to the previous scene.

- At other points in the play, Scarlet steps forward and talks to the audience. Her conversations mostly concern her fractured childhood and her sexual exploits.

- Her very close friendship with Lucy. They are like sisters.

- Lucy and Scarlet grew up in much the same disturbed environment, but they differ in their responses to it. This is particularly evident in their reaction to Mick's pornography and how they feel about sex in general. These childhood reactions are subsequently carried through into their adult lives and continue to be a source of difference between them in the play.

- The speech serves to fill in the backstory for the audience and allows us to view the main action with a greater degree of understanding. In this sense, Scarlet becomes more than just a character. She is also the 'storyteller'. Make a decision about why she personally needs to tell us these things (might it be to do with her loneliness? Or the fact that her parents never listened to her or took her seriously?) so that the speech is triggered by a strong need on her part (and not just there to beef up the story).

☞ **WHAT SHE WANTS**

- To shed some light on her relationship and shared history with Lucy and Mick.

- To recall and describe her complete loss of innocence.

- To explain her cynicism.

☞ **KEYWORDS** *(there are many)* crap bullying bastard repulsive lizard black anger despising darkness/dark hole

☞ **NB** This play offers a number of other speeches from which to choose.

Scarlet

" Lucy and I used to play Crap Family Poker. Lucy would call a Bullying-Father and a Mother-On-Valium, and I'd match her Mother-On-Valium and raise her a Bastard-Stepfather-Who-Charges-Me-Rent. Although, when I was thirteen he put it up to more than I could earn with a Saturday job, so [...] I went to live with Lucy.

It was a funny set-up. Mick was never there or when he was he was just drunk the whole time [...] and Lucy's mum, Geraldine, was always round the cooker as if for warmth [...] or whispering into the phone – *obviously* having an affair [...]

Lucy and I were not exactly your well-adjusted teenagers at the time. She was in her gothic we're-all-going-to-die-of-AIDS phase and I was just more interested in... planting a bomb in my mother's tampon, I suppose.

We'd pass on the landing in the mornings, me on my way to be sick after binge-eating too much cereal, and her on her way to steal money from her dad's wallet.

Lucy hated Mick. Or rather, I think she tried to hate him because he never really took any notice of her. Except to say 'Don't like boys too much, you're better off on your own'. I think she thought it was her *fault* somehow. Then she found his stash of porn magazines that were full of tall, pouty women with big tits and somehow took it as an explanation [...] so Lucy would steal his money, and then she'd go on huge shopping sprees and buy... oh I don't know... *clothes*... Mostly she never wore them or she'd just throw them away [...]

So this one morning Lucy's in a snit because her dad's got up early for once, *avec* wallet, so she comes downstairs for breakfast but her dad bangs into her and tells her she can't come down like that – what if one of his friends came round?

Course, Mick's just freaked out at having a teenage daughter on the loose with no knickers on, no matter how long her dressing gown is, but Lucy immediately takes it as final proof that she's too repulsive to be seen in public, so she comes running back upstairs and shoves her face in a line of my speed to take the edge off things.

I thought of going to her, but at that point I was still cross because she'd shrunk my new top so...

Anyway, so the big scene between Lucy and Mick gives Geraldine the perfect excuse to pick a fight so she can nip out for a quick one, so she throws a hissy fit [...] and storms out, saying she's had enough of the lot of them and isn't ever coming back. Which starts Lucy off crying and screaming and...

Which, of course, is really hard to wank through, so I finally give up and come out onto the landing to see if I can help. I bump into a lodger, a grey-skinned man with eyes like a lizard, carrying a suitcase. He tells me he's leaving. All this shouting is too much to put up with. [...] I see him look me up and down, and I know what he's thinking. And Geraldine's been good to me and she needs the money.

Penises are strange. On one level, mechanics. But on the other, a manifest wanting of me. And it's the wanting that sucks me in, holding it up to the light like a marble, to look at, in awe, this penis-shaped wanting of me.

And while he grunts in the darkness, lost in his skin, I gaze at my marble. And later, I have black acorns in my stomach, acorns of anger and despising how easily that desire for me was sated. And I plant them and watch them grow into big dark trees hiding me from the light.

Downstairs the front door goes as Geraldine comes back. The grey-skinned lodger strokes my skin, eyeing up the one remaining hole he hasn't been in. 'You dirty girl,' he whispers. 'You've got "Fuck me" written all over you. You want me in here, don't you?' 'Yes,' I lie. But what I'm really thinking is, it's seven o'clock. Which means I've missed dinner. **99**

Apologia

Alexi Kaye Campbell

☞ **WHO**   Claire, thirties, an actress.

☞ **TO WHOM**   Kristin, sixties, an art historian and the mother of Claire's boyfriend, Simon.

☞ **WHERE**   The kitchen of Kristin's cottage somewhere in the English countryside.

☞ **WHEN**   Present day.

☞ **WHAT HAS JUST HAPPENED**   Kristin is a celebrated art historian. She holds strong feminist and left-wing views and throughout her adult life has been a staunch campaigner and political activist. She has recently published a book of memoirs but has omitted to mention that she has two sons. When Peter, her eldest, and then Simon, her youngest, arrive to celebrate her birthday, the now grown-up men confront their mother about the way in which she has neglected them. Claire, Simon's girlfriend, is an actress. She has a regular part in a popular television series that Kristin regards as 'the biggest pile of putrid shite I have ever seen in my life'. During the course of the evening, Kristin goads Claire, criticising her about the vacuousness of her professional and personal choices. Claire is wearing a dress that cost seven hundred pounds. Trudi, Peter's girlfriend, accidentally spills red wine on it. Here, the morning after, Claire confronts Kristin. She and Simon are splitting up and she wants to say goodbye. The following speech is made up of Claire's part of their conversation.

☞ **WHAT TO CONSIDER**

- Claire has had to turn down theatre work in order to appear in the soap. Decide to what extent her 'artist' self feels compromised by her decision to make money and by her desire for fame.

- She insists the series is 'a clever and profound piece of television'. Is that what she really thinks?

- She drives a BMW and wears designer clothes.

- She has been cheating on Simon.

- The courage it might take, talking to Kristin in this way.

- The jump from: 'How do you do that?' to: 'Did I ever tell you about my father?' needs a quick change of thought. In the unedited text it is also quite sudden, and only separated by Kristin saying: 'I really wouldn't know.'

☞ WHAT SHE WANTS

- To assert herself and to defend herself from Kristin's attack.

- To explain her past in order to justify her present.

- To reveal to Kristin the truth about her (Kristin's) limitations.

☞ KEYWORDS stifled blood stains carapace demonise vilify scrutinise condemn

Claire

❝ I don't think I'll be seeing you again. […] So I thought it only right to say goodbye. Consider it a mark of respect.

Pause.

I don't know what you and Simon talked about last night. But when he came back to the room he woke me up and we chatted till dawn. You'll be happy to hear we've decided to part ways. […] Don't flatter yourself into believing that it was your doing. It was inevitable. We've just been putting it off, that's all. I'm surprised we lasted for a year and a half. […] He said he realised the only reason he was attracted to me was because I was the polar opposite of you. […] It's funny. When you said last night that you thought I was good in *A Doll's House*, my heart missed a beat. I nearly leapt for joy. How do you do that? […] Did I ever tell you about my father? […] I watched him slowly drown in a mountain of unpaid bills. When I was thirteen he was declared bankrupt. I used to come home every day after school and the bathroom door was always closed and the sound was always the same – the sound of my mother's stifled sobs. Then she'd come out with a smile on her face and cook dinner. One day, he left and never came back. My mother and I moved to a small rented flat and lived on benefits. The first day I moved my bed and there was a whole lot of blood on the wall. I spent all my time in that flat wondering what had happened before we arrived. I came up with quite a few upsetting scenarios. I had a vivid imagination.

Pause.

Since then most of my life I've been running away from unpaid bills, stifled sobs and those dark-red stains. That may have affected some of my artistic choices.

Pause.

That's my individual story. But something tells me that somewhere along the line you've stopped listening to people's individual stories. I wonder when that happened.

Pause. She waits for something from KRISTIN *but nothing comes.*

There's a part of me that admires you. The way you've held onto the things you've believed in. But your idealism has turned into hardness, Kristin. It has a thick, thick shell. You do. A carapace. Isn't that the word? [...] 'Why does she demonise me like that?' I kept asking myself. 'Why does she vilify me? Why does she scrutinise everything I do and then condemn it without a second thought?' [...] And then I decided it's got nothing to do with me really. It's not about me. [...] It's about you, Kristin. [...] When I was in my room last night I had a little bit of a revelation. [...] They say, don't they, that when people get older they just become worse versions of themselves. [...] Maybe in some people that's a little more pronounced. [...] And I expect it's really a case of having to hold onto everything you are. Everything you *were*. The choices you made, the paths you followed. Because if you start to question them, if you start to doubt them… well, then you're fucked really, aren't you? [...] So you hang on with every fibre of your being.

Pause.

It must be exhausting being you. **"**

August: Osage County
Tracy Letts

☞ **WHO**   Jean, fourteen, Midwestern American.

☞ **TO WHOM**   Johnna, housekeeper, twenty-six, Native American.

☞ **WHERE**   The attic room of Jean's grandparents house in Oklahoma.

☞ **WHEN**   August 2007.

☞ **WHAT HAS JUST HAPPENED**   The speech comes near the beginning of the play. Jean's grandfather Beverly has gone missing. Family members including Barbara and Bill, Jean's parents, return with Jean to the family home to help out. Before he went, Beverly employed Johnna to work as housekeeper. She is sleeping in the attic where Jean used to stay when she came to visit. Now Jean is sleeping next to her grandmother Violet's room. Jean wants to smoke pot and the attic room is the safest place.

☞ **WHAT TO CONSIDER**

- Jean is fourteen, but when asked she lies and says she is fifteen. To what extent has she lost her innocence?

- She is an only child and the only grandchild of Beverly and Violet. How lonely is she?

- Her eccentricity. She is a film buff and loves old black-and-white movies. She is a vegetarian.

- She likes to shock, but it is important to note that the use of 'bad language' is common in the family.

- Make a decision about whether you will mime smoking the pipe, or use a real object (see note on using props in the introduction). Remember, that owing to our public smoking ban, you will have to pretend to light and smoke it.

☞ **WHAT SHE WANTS**

- To dull her pain. To what extent does Jean use pot as a way of avoiding her unhappy feelings?

- Company. Johnna is the closest person in age to her. Note how quick she is to talk about her parents and all that is aggravating her.

- To prove that she is mature and that she can cope with all that is happening. To what extent is this a front?

☞ **KEYWORDS**   bugging   trouble   sweating   bad   cool   uncool   dicks   fucking   turd   sucks   hawk   freak-out   addict   shoot

Jean

❝ Hi. […] Am I bugging you? […] No, I thought maybe you'd like to smoke a bowl with me? […] Okay. I didn't know. Am I bugging you? […] Okay. Do you mind if I smoke a bowl? […] 'Cause there's no place I can go. Y'know, I'm staying right by Grandma's room, and if I go outside, they're gonna wonder – […] Mom and Dad don't mind. You won't get into trouble or anything. […] Okay. You sure?

From her pocket, JEAN *takes a small glass pipe and a clear cigarette wrapper holding a bud of marijuana. She fixes the pipe.*

I say they don't mind. If they knew I stuck this bud under the cap of Dad's deodorant before our flight and then sat there sweating like in that movie *Maria Full of Grace*. Did you see that? […] I just mean they don't mind that I smoke pot. Dad doesn't. Mom kind of does. She thinks it's bad for me. I think the real reason it bugs her is 'cause Dad smokes pot, too, and she wishes he didn't. Dad's much cooler than Mom, really. Well, that's not true. He's just cooler in that way, I guess.

JEAN *smokes. She offers the smouldering pipe to* JOHNNA.

(*Holding her breath.*) You sure? […] No, he's really not cooler. (*Exhales smoke.*) He and Mom are separated right now. […] He's fucking one of his students which is pretty uncool, if you ask me. Some people would think that's cool, like those dicks who teach with him in the Humanities Department because they're all fucking their students or wish they were fucking their students. 'Lo–liii–ta.' I mean, I don't care and all, he can fuck whoever he wants and he's a teacher and that's who teachers meet, students. He was just a turd the way he went about it and didn't give Mom a chance to respond or anything. What sucks now is that Mom's watching me like a hawk, like, she's afraid I'll have some post-divorce freak-out and become some heroin addict or shoot everybody at school. Or God forbid, lose my virginity. I don't know what it is about Dad splitting that put Mom on hymen patrol. Do you have a boyfriend? […] Me neither. I did go with this boy Josh for like almost a year but he was retarded. Are your parents still together? […] Oh. I'm sorry. […] Oh, fuck, no, I'm really sorry, I feel fucking terrible now. […] Oh God. Okay. Were you close with them? […] Okay, another stupid question there, Jean, real good. Wow. Like: 'Are you close to your parents?' […] Yeah, right? So that's what I meant. Thanks. **99**

☞ **NB**   You will have to imagine Johnna's responses to Jean's two questions, 'Are your parents still together?' and 'Were you close with them?', in order for the speech to flow. Where there are now brackets […] to denote a cut, the unedited text reads as follows:

JEAN. Are your parents still together?

JOHNNA. They passed away.

JEAN. Oh. I'm sorry.

JOHNNA. That's okay. Thank you.

JEAN. Oh, fuck, no, I'm really sorry, I feel fucking terrible now.

JOHNNA. It's okay.

JEAN. Oh God. Okay. Were you close with them?

JOHNNA. Yeah.

JEAN. Okay, another stupid question there, Jean, real good. Wow. Like: 'Are you close to your parents?'

JOHNNA. Not everybody is.

JEAN. Yeah, right? So that's what I meant. Thanks.

bedbound

Enda Walsh

☞ **WHO**   Daughter, a young woman, crippled, from Cork, in Southern Ireland.

☞ **TO WHOM**   Herself.

☞ **WHERE**   Her bed. In a house in Cork, Ireland.

☞ **WHEN**   Present day.

☞ **WHAT HAS JUST HAPPENED**   The play tells the story of the relationship between a daughter, crippled by polio, and her father, a furniture salesman and psychotic murderer. They speak from a small child's bed, which they share. The bed is surrounded by plasterboard walls that the father erected after his daughter contracted the polio. At the very start of the play the wall closest to the audience falls away, thus inviting us into their world. While the main thrust of the father's conversation is about his past achievements and then thwarted ambitions, the daughter speaks to shut out the terrifying silence in her head. Here in this speech she recalls the day she contracted the polio.

☞ **WHAT TO CONSIDER**

- The play's themes are dark and its content brutal. Read it to understand fully the relationship between father and daughter and to experience the surprise tenderness of its ending.

- The style is heightened and non-naturalistic. The language, poetic.

- The daughter's physicality. Make a decision about how you will portray her handicap. We also know from the stage directions that 'her face is filthy, her hair tangled and manky'.

- Of all the daughter's speeches, this is the most simple and clear, reflecting a time in her life when the world was relatively normal.

- Her mother is dead. We presume she has been killed by the father.

☞ WHAT SHE WANTS

- To shut out her father's presence.
- To relive a time when she was just an ordinary little girl.
- To remember her mother.
- To escape momentarily the madness of her present situation.

☞ KEYWORDS   (*there are many*) fire   shimmering   tippled
scrunched   squeezed   healthy   crippled   sucked   squatted
squished   spitting   springing   shit   puke   mad

Daughter

❝ I'll speak the only thing that's clear to me just ta shut you
out. I remember I fire meself out of this bed and sling my ten-
year-old bikini on.

DAD *tries to hide under the blanket. She continues with conviction.*

It's all yellow with pink dots and I fasten it around my chest…
as if I had anything to hide. I've got awful problems fastening
the bikini but then feel the long fingers of Mam click me into
shape and pat me on the head. I smell the hand cream on her
fingers. I look at her fingers made rough from all the pastry.
All those millions of vol-au-vents turning her hands to cake.
All for you and that fucking shop. I tell her that she's beautiful
because to me she is. As usual she stays quiet and we get the
bus to the beach with the summer heat sending the bus
shimmering towards our stop. 'Might Dad one day blow up,
Mam?' I think that was the question I asked. And she started
to laugh. The people on the bus turned and smiled because
her laugh was so loud and happy. I had a good old laugh
meself thinking of you blowing up in our new fitted kitchen all
over the Formica worktops. In my laugh I let a fart which
made Mam laugh even louder. All laughed out we lay in the
water as the tide tippled up over us and both looking up
towards the sun. Scrunched-up faces. I turned over and lay on
Mam and kissed the salt off her face. The dry sea salt on her

beautiful face like she were a frosted bun I told her. And then she hugged me so hard it almost squeezed the air out of my inflatable-swan ring. That was nice. And that's when I went for a walk. I left Mam lying on the beach. That would be the last time I would see her as a healthy girl. I walked over the dunes spying on the teenagers snatching at their crotches. I talked to a priest sunbathing with the Bible and his crippled mother who sucked on oranges like they were going out of fashion. He read the story about Jesus in the desert to me and squatted a wasp with the Gospel of St John. Squished it dead. I walked on pretending that I was Jesus in search of water with only hours to live. I pretended I was a desert rabbit and ran through the sharp rushes like a right mad yoke. The rushes like nasty pins and needles firing me faster and faster and faster and faster. The soft sand sent spitting from my heels. My skinny arms and legs a mad blur. My springy hair springing out straight from my speed. My head free. Free of you and that fucking furniture talk. And then I felt no ground underneath me. Like the dog in the Roadrunner cartoons I tried running in the air. It was sort of funny until I fell down. And I fell down into this big hole. And right up to my waist I was covered in shit. I soon stopped trying to catch any clean air and just breathed in the shit air. I had a little puke. Puked up the cola bottles I ate on the bus. I wiped my mouth of the puke with a hand covered in shit. I spat the shit out and started to climb up a little ladder out of the concrete hole. And I didn't even cry. And that's the story of the day I got the polio. From then on everything went mad, didn't it? And ya know a day doesn't go past where I think I should have stayed in that place. How fucking happy I'd be. **99**

Boys

Ella Hickson

☞ **WHO**   Sophie, graduating student, middle class, from Southern England.

☞ **TO WHOM**   Mack, her secret lover.

☞ **WHERE**   The kitchen of a student flat in Edinburgh.

☞ **WHEN**   Present day, summer.

☞ **WHAT HAS JUST HAPPENED**   Mack, Cam, Timp and Benny share a flat in Edinburgh. It is the end of term, Mack and Benny are graduating and the contract is up on their flat. The boys have been partying. The festivities continue the following evening when the boys are joined by Timp's girlfriend Laura and Sophie, who we soon understand is having a secret relationship with Mack. It becomes apparent that Sophie used to go out with Benny's brother Peter. Peter has recently hanged himself. During the course of the evening Sophie confesses to Laura that she is in love with Mack and that it was while she was still with Peter that she started seeing him. She explains to Laura that Mack had told her that before anything could happen between them she would have to choose between him and Peter. Laura then makes the connection between Peter's suicide and Sophie's choice. Immediately after this conversation with Laura, Mack enters and in a snatched moment between them Sophie broaches the subject.

☞ **WHAT TO CONSIDER**

- The play takes place over a twenty-four-hour period.

- It is hot and the dustbins have not been cleared. The smell of rotting rubbish permeates the scenes.

- Inside, the action is fuelled by drugs and alcohol.

- Outside, while the flatmates are revelling, a riot is taking place.

☞ **WHAT SHE WANTS**

- To confess to her lack of feeling about Peter's suicide.

- To gain reassurance that she is not a bad person.

- To justify her happiness in the wake of someone else's misery.

- To profess her love to Mack. Note how vulnerable this leaves her.

- To understand what it means to love and to be loved.

- To illicit a response from Mack. (For him to tell her that he loves her, thereby making it all all right.)

☞ **KEYWORDS**   guilt   grief   feel   joy   peace

Sophie

❝ Do you; have you ever actually felt any – guilt? Because it's come as a bit of a surprise that um, that – you, one, I don't, can't actually feel it. Like I can't get my body to do it, on its own, it's not something I can generate somehow, like, I – I find myself having to actually summon it, trying to encourage myself, to summon it and even then I can't do it, really, I can't feel it. I thought it might be shock at first and then – grief or but I think I might not feel it. I can't. I don't. All I can feel is total joy, total – peace. I look at you and I sometimes actually make myself think of him, I force him into my head and I don't feel guilty. What does that mean? What kind of person does that make me? (*Pause.*) Hm? Sometimes I think it's because – what we have is love, meant to be. (*Laughs.*) That we love each other, yes, Mack, that is what I sometimes think. Is that ridiculous? And sometimes I even think that that love is so important that it is bigger, or equal to – what he did. That they are just two feelings, one is love and the other is despair and both just have an action. And that those actions are different but that somehow they are equal – does that make me a monster? I sat at his funeral looking at his parents and Benny but all I could think of, all I could feel – was you.

But then I look at you and I wonder if it's actually there. I wonder if I added up the amount of minutes, hours, fucking days I have spent thinking about you, the amount of fucking longing I have done – if I added that up and weighed it against anything you have ever actually said… and – (*Pause.*)

But then you do the smallest thing you make me a cup of tea when I don't ask, or you touch my hand really lightly in a room full of people and I think no, Sophie, don't laugh – don't laugh because it's real and it's so much more real because it's unsaid and unspoken and un – un – un – it's so much more real because I can't touch it, because we can't say it and I can't see it, it's so much more real because I don't know if it's there.

Pause. MACK *doesn't say anything.*

Please say something. (*Pause.*) Please. Please tell me if…

She trails off unable to try any harder. **99**

Brontë

Polly Teale

☞ **WHO**   Anne, twenty-eight.

☞ **TO WHOM**   Charlotte, her sister.

☞ **WHERE**   The kitchen of the Parsonage at Haworth on the Yorkshire Moors.

☞ **WHEN**   Autumn 1848, shortly after the death of her brother Branwell.

☞ **WHAT HAS JUST HAPPENED**   The play depicts incidents both real and imaginary in the lives of the Brontë sisters and their brother Branwell. It moves backwards and forwards in time and is intermixed with characters from the Brontës' novels. At this point in the play, Charlotte is enjoying much literary success following the publication of *Jane Eyre*. Anne and Charlotte travel to London, but on their return their brother Branwell dies. A short time later, while Anne is sorting through Branwell's clothes, Charlotte, who is trying to write, complains of the pressure she feels to deliver a second and further outstanding piece of work. The speech is made up of Anne's response to this and then supplemented by a passage she has a few lines later in which she questions their need to write at all.

☞ **WHAT TO CONSIDER**

- Anne wrote *Agnes Grey* and *The Tenant of Wildfell Hall*. Reading her novels will give you greater insight.

- Anne's writing was more socially and politically motivated than her sisters. She had a keen sense of injustice and was particularly concerned about poor working conditions. As Polly Teale points out in her introduction to the play, this was a time of great social upheaval. The Industrial Revolution was underway, and Anne would have witnessed many changes.

- She views the need to write and to be heard as something of a sickness.

- Unless it is able to bring about change, Anne considers her art to be pointless.

- The sisters are grieving the loss of their brother Branwell. His death and the circumstances surrounding it are the 'recent events' to which she refers.

- Charlotte has paid for Branwell's funeral and cleared all his debts with the money she had received from her publisher.

- Branwell was a complex man. He suffered many addictions, was an alcoholic and died aged thirty-one.

- Their mother died when Anne was barely one year old, which goes some way to explaining her and her siblings' make-up.

- Keighley is pronounced 'Keethly'.

☞ WHAT SHE WANTS

- To protect her sister.

- To open Charlotte's eyes to a different way of living that involves simple tasks and pleasures so that they may achieve peace and contentment.

- To create value and to be useful to society.

- To belong to something bigger than herself. Note how she longs to be part of a busy workforce.

- To question and to understand their restlessness. 'Why is it not enough to be?' Perhaps you may like to draw on your own feelings and attitude to acting in order to understand this need to be heard. I would suggest that it is not that much different.

☞ KEYWORDS   renounce   honest   practicality   afflicted
thrum   activity   labours   use

Anne

❝ Do you ever wonder what our lives would have been had we never put pen to paper? Had we never been afflicted by that curious condition which must have you turn life into words. Yesterday, coming back from Keighley through the wood, I was looking at the trees, at the autumn light, and trying to describe it, for it is autumn in my story, when I came upon the blackberry-pickers. They sang as they worked. There's not a soul amongst them can read or write and yet I thought I would give anything to be one of them, to be part of that great thrum of life and activity. To see the fruit of your labours in front of you at the end of the day and to know that it will be of use to others. They stopped when they saw me watching. They took off their hats and nodded and I knew that they wanted me gone. It was not a performance. The singing was not for me or anyone else. It was for its own sake. Like breathing, they did it without knowing. They didn't need anyone to hear. (*Pause.*) Why do we need someone to hear us? Why is it not enough to be? [...] Why do we do it? [...] Why us? Why always? As far back as I remember. [...] I used to think we could change things. That by telling the truth we would make a better world. [...] There are people living in poverty, terrible injustice and suffering and we... we write. [...] What do we want? What is it for? **❞**

Bull

Mike Bartlett

☞ **WHO**   Isobel, a young professional.

☞ **TO WHOM**   Thomas, her ex-colleague.

☞ **WHERE**   An office.

☞ **WHEN**   Present day.

☞ **WHAT HAS JUST HAPPENED**   Isobel and her two male colleagues, Thomas and Tony, wait for their boss Carter to arrive. Carter is performing an office 'cull' and will sack one of them today. In order to safeguard their positions, Isobel and Tony have ganged up on Thomas. They bully him and convince Carter that Thomas is the one who should be fired. The speech that follows comes at the very end of the play following Thomas's dismissal.

☞ WHAT TO CONSIDER

- The insecurity of the job market and the brutality of the workplace.

- In the original production the set resembled a boxing or wrestling ring.

- The play makes reference to and is reminiscent of *The Apprentice*.

- Isobel is described variously as 'a bitch', 'icy', 'frozen', 'hard', 'tight' and 'anal'.

- She says she is like that because she was sexually abused by her father. Thomas maintains that she is lying. You decide.

- When she says she feels sorry for him, is it genuine, or is it mocking?

- Make a decision about why she chooses to tell him all this. She could just as easily have left it.

- What might she gain from going in for the kill in this way, and what does it suggest about the world in which she lives?

- Note the unusual layout of the speech. First, short sentences each given their own line, followed by two/three longish paragraphs. What might this suggest about her thought patterns and what happens to her when she gets into her stride?

☞ **WHAT SHE WANTS**

- To flatten Thomas.
- To crush him.
- To kill in order to survive.

☞ **KEYWORDS**   tough   shit   ex   crucial

☞ **NB**   This play offers a number of other speeches from which to choose.

Isobel

❝ I feel really sorry for you. […]

No Thomas I feel *really* sorry. I do. I promise. I do. I'm feeling sorrow. Right now.

You have a kid don't you?

You do.

I know you do.

So.

So you don't need to hide it.

You have a kid.

[…]

Yeah. Tough. What's its name?

Is it Harry?

It is Harry.

I know it is.

You know how I know this?

It's because once when we left work, I was walking behind you and you walked all the way down the road, and I could see you in front of me, and I saw you meet this woman in a coffee shop it wasn't a nice coffee shop I was surprised you went into it, it was a Costa or something not even a good one a shit Costa, and I watched you meet this woman and she had a little toddling little thing, and I waited and I saw you go to the loo, and then I ran in and said oh I was hoping to catch you and I pretended I was in a hurry, and I had a little chat with Marion, is that her name your ex and she told me about Harry, and I said I was a colleague and you were taking ages in the toilet actually we talked about it we didn't know what you were up to in there, but it meant we had a good talk about you, and in the end when you still didn't come out I said I needed to dash and I'd catch you tomorrow instead, but that conversation with her gave me quite a lot of crucial information.

Which I've always known when you've tried to hide things or lie or whatever, I've always known about your life things that you don't know I know. I know you have to pay Marion that certain amount every month and when she hears that you're out of work her low estimation of you will drop even further it will I promise she won't be surprised that's the really tragic thing for you, she won't be like oh my God you lost your job! Oh my God! She'll be like, yeah of course he lost his job fucking retard good thing I got out while I could, better not let him see Harry too much don't want Harry to grow up in the distorted disabled image of his fucking drip drip of a father.

I expect that's what she'll think.

It's tough isn't it, life.

Is it a lot more difficult than you imagined it would be?

I mean I'm sure you thought it was difficult but that through sheer hard work, and practice and training and long hours and inspiration and in your case perspiration you would come through and in the end, succeed, because you thought that despite everything, it was, in this country at least, a meritocracy and that fair play and honest, transparent behaviour at work would be rewarded in the end. That bad people like me would fall at the wayside and good people like you would triumph.

That's what you thought isn't it?

Oops. **"**

Bunny

Jack Thorne

☞ **WHO**   Katie, eighteen, from Luton.

☞ **TO WHOM**   The audience (see note on 'Direct audience address' in the introduction).

☞ **WHERE**   Various locations in Luton.

☞ **WHEN**   Present day.

☞ **WHAT HAS JUST HAPPENED**   Katie has met her older boyfriend Abe, a twenty-four-year-old black man, at the school gates. It is a hot day, and Abe goes to buy an ice cream. As he eats it walking down the street, a boy on a bicycle comes past and knocks his ice cream out of his hand. Abe reacts instinctively and kicks the wheels of the bike, sending the boy flying. A fight then breaks out between the two with Katie looking on in surprise. She then somewhat randomly tells us about how she envies the way fat people can eat with abandon.

☞ **WHAT TO CONSIDER**

- The whole play is one long monologue. In it, Katie tells the story of what happened that afternoon. The events are interwoven with reminiscences of further episodes in her life largely to do with family, boyfriends and school.

- The 'story' is told in the present tense as if it were happening to her now. This creates dramatic tension. When she steps out of the narrative to recall other events, she reverts to the past tense. Whichever passage from the play you choose to perform, make a decision about where you might be. See yourself on the street as she describes it or (later on in her story) in the car, at the butcher's, in the stranger's house, etc. You might like to imagine that the passages delivered in the past tense are told from a different location. Perhaps from the comfort of her bedroom.

- It is hot weather. How does this influence her behaviour? What effect does it have on the men around her?

☞ **WHAT SHE WANTS**

- Attention.

- To shock us with her lack of political correctness. Throughout the play Katie uses language and expresses opinions that are designed to provoke a reaction. To what extent do you think she enjoys playing the rebel?

- To show how adult and mature she is. She is very frank about her sexual exploits, even her failures.

- To create an impression that she is tough, and that she doesn't give a damn. To what extent is this a front? A way of talking and being that shields her vulnerability? Note how she uses humour to laugh off otherwise painful experiences.

- To figure out who she is and what it is she wants, independently of her parents, boyfriend, friends and teachers. Note how she describes herself as 'the unfit fitter'.

- To shake off the schoolgirl and to become a woman.

☞ **KEYWORDS**   gratitude   awesome   friend/friends   unfit   Illustrative   funny   complicated

☞ **NB**   This play offers a number of other speeches from which to choose.

Katie

❝ I used to have a fat friend. Sheridan. Named after a Sheffield Wednesday footballer – and they wondered why she ate? Bulimia in the end. She got hospitalised once she turned yellow. Then they moved her from the school – when she got out – of hospital – because they wanted to 'change her routine' and they weren't sure our school was a 'healthy environment'. Like any school is a healthy environment. But I did like watching her eat. With every mouthful you just saw this look of pure gratitude crossing her face – like – I can't believe I'm getting to eat this… this is awesome.

I say 'friend'. She wasn't really. My friends are different. I'm
– difficult to explain without sounding thick – but me and her
don't fit like that. Not that I fit anywhere. I'm the unfit fitter. I
don't fit. But not in a bad way. Just in a – way. To give an
instance – and this is true – and very very illustrative –
everyone came to my eighteenth-birthday party – I mean,
every single one of the twenty-five I invited – and all were
important – but also everyone left my birthday party – every
single one of the twenty-five – at 10.30 p.m.

Which is not a normal time to leave any birthday party, I
know. And that's what I mean about…

But they were bored and it was quite shit and they thought
it'd be quite funny to leave, and it sort of was, you know?
Funny. Still quite an embarrassing one to explain to your
parents. Where are all your friends? Um. Hiding. No.
They've gone. Obviously. Where have they gone? Um.
Home. Probably. Why? Why have they gone? Turn. Look
parents in the eye. Because this was pointless. I basically
turned it all on them. Which was fair enough. They'd made
some effort. But the wrong effort. And so had I. I mean, it
was mostly my fault. There was booze – but there were too
many snacks and not enough Ann Summers' toys or
something. I don't know.

Anyway, it's not as bad as it sounds…

Still. Mum apologised a week later for it being crap. But she
didn't do it well enough. So I stole her wallet. She spent ages
looking for it. 'I know I must have left it somewhere.' Turned
the house upside down. Had to cancel all her cards. And being
Mum and slightly overcautious about most things, cancelling
all her cards included cancelling her library card – 'I just don't
want to accrue unnecessary fines, that's all.' She said.

I put it in her sock drawer two days later. Minus one pound
fifty exactly just to see if she'd notice. She didn't. She was
pleased. To get it back.

Anyway, that's… what's complicated. That's part of my
resettlement software.

Abe didn't come to the party. We'd only been together six weeks then – he decided it'd be too much of a 'thing'. That's when we had sex actually. That night. After he decided he couldn't come to my birthday party because it was too much of a commitment I decided that I'd give him my Virginia County. **99**

Cockroach

Sam Holcroft

☞ **WHO**   Mmoma, teenager, black, born in Britain to Nigerian parents.

☞ **TO WHOM**   A soldier's uniform that she pretends is a real man.

☞ **WHERE**   A classroom in a school.

☞ **WHEN**   Present day or possibly the near future, as the country is at war.

☞ **WHAT HAS JUST HAPPENED**   Lee, Leah, Danielle, Davey and Mmoma are all in detention. Their exams are coming up in four weeks, and their teacher Beth is determined to use the time for biology revision. Every afternoon, once school has finished, the five gather in the classroom where they learn about evolution, genetic variation and natural selection. Outside there is a war raging and young men are being called up to join the army. Two weeks later, the school is put forward by the headmistress to help with the war effort, and boxes of soldiers' uniforms arrive to be recycled. Mmoma is desperate for a boyfriend. She has already tried unsuccessfully to get off with Lee and Davey (who are going out with Leah and Danielle respectively) but, due to the conflict, there are fewer and fewer young men around. 'Where am I going to get a boyfriend from? There's, like, three girls to every one boy left in this school.' The next best thing is the soldier's uniform which Mmoma hangs on a line and then talks to as if 'he' were real.

☞ **WHAT TO CONSIDER**

- Mmoma feels herself to be the outsider. She is the only black person in the group and the only one without a boyfriend or girlfriend. She is terrified of insignificance.

- Her hormones are raging and she is eager for sex.

- She is provocative and flirtatious.

- Despite being in detention she is a diligent student. We know from Beth that she is intelligent, inquisitive and could be a scientist. Interestingly, Mmoma wants to be a musician and singer. To what extent is this to do with her need for attention?

☞ WHAT SHE WANTS

- To be noticed.
- To be wanted.
- To feel special.
- To be made love to and to be loved.
- To satisfy her physical and emotional hunger.

☞ KEYWORDS   exotic   wide   sweet   big   blush   beautiful   strong   black   belly   gut   head

Mmoma

❝ What? […]

My name?

Oh. Um. Mmoma.

Mmoma Ejiofor.

Oh, thank you. Yes, it is exotic. Nigerian. Africa.

The great wide Africa.

No, I never been. But. I'm going to. Going to go to Nigeria, Africa. Step off the plane and be like, 'I'm home…'

What was that? Oh, you think so? You're sweet.

What my, my eyes? Yes, they are big.

She touches her hair.

Oh, thank you. I had it done.

She looks down at her body.

Oh don't, you'll make me blush. Well, I do try to keep myself in shape. I don't eat all junk and –

She covers her behind, shocked.

'Scuse me, I don't think you should even be looking there.

Shame on you. What are you like?

Tut. Tut. Tut.

She turns away and surreptitiously shows him her bottom.

Sorry, what was that?

She turns back.

No. I'm still at school.

Why, did you think I was older?

I get that a lot.

I never get ID'd, never, not even at Price Smart on the High Street, and they're, like, well strict –

What, sorry?

You what? You want to know everything?

Everything there is to know? About me?

Well. My gosh. Where to start…?

What do I wanna be? When I grow up?

I'm actually quite grown up already.

But, when I leave school? Well. My mum wants me to be a doctor. Everyone wants me to try and get to be a doctor or a pharmacist or… But. Really. Deep, right deep down, in me. Is a singer!

That's right. I'm gonna be a musician!

My inspiration?

Shirley. Shirley Bassey: the most greatest singer that ever was!

The most beautiful strong black British daughter-of-a-Nigerian singing woman – that is gonna be me! **99**

Dancing Bears*

Sam Holcroft

☞ **WHO**   Charity, fifteen.

☞ **TO WHOM**   Aaron, her brother.

☞ **WHERE**   Exact place unspecified, but 'the stage floor is alive with red-hot coals'.

☞ **WHEN**   Present day.

☞ **WHAT HAS JUST HAPPENED**   Aaron, Charity's brother, has been explaining to the audience why the Brazilians are so much better at football than the English. Then three other boys, first Dean, then Retard, and finally Angry, arrive on stage. They join in the chat about football, share a bottle of vodka, which dulls the pain of the red-hot coals underfoot, and are generally larking about. But when Angry tells the group about how a girl was violently raped things soon take a savage turn, and the boys start fighting over chicken nuggets, vying for position within the gang. Angry and Retard fight. As Angry releases Retard and Retard twists in pain, he (Retard) removes his sweat shirt 'revealing the feminine curves of her body'. In this way, Retard becomes Charity, Aaron's sister, and she has something she wants to tell him.

☞ **WHAT TO CONSIDER**

- The main body of the speech is written and delivered in one. Where I have inserted […] two thirds down, is where the speech is supplemented by a passage picked up from another part of the play and joined together to make it longer.

- The play is very physical. Dean, Retard and Angry all become girls who form a gang, much like that of the boys.

- The play is part of a collection of six plays called *Charged*, and was commissioned by Clean Break theatre company, who work with women whose lives have been affected by the criminal justice system.

* Published in the volume *Charged*

- Both Charity and Aaron try to remain outside the gang. To what extent does this leave them weak and vulnerable to attack?

- Make a decision about what the floor of red-hot coals might represent.

☞ **WHAT SHE WANTS**

- To ensure that Aaron listens to the story of the baby fox. It has had a huge impact on her. Decide to what extent it is a metaphor for her own feelings of helplessness.

- To figure out why it has affected her so much. Even the memory of watching a grown man being beaten to death has had less of an impact. Note how this bothers her. Decide to what extent she has become so brutalised that she is numb to certain events.

☞ **KEYWORDS**   baby   tiny   jumped   running   blood   stain wild   twisted   fire

Charity

❝ Aaron? […] I was in a car at the traffic lights and I saw across the other side of the road a baby fox. […] It had run out from someone's front garden and it was so tiny it could hardly walk on its little legs. […] But it bounded across the pavement like Bambi and ran into the road just as the lights changed and the car in front took off. […] And my heart, like, jumped into my throat all of a sudden but the car stopped and I thought, 'Thank God, it's stopped just in time,' and I was waiting for it to run out the other side but I couldn't see it and then the car in front swerved and drove around it and I could see that it was still running, the baby fox, but running on its side with his head now facing its tail and blood coming from its mouth with these wild, wild eyes. And though I only saw it for a second I can't stop seeing the image in my mind. And when we drove past again on the way back it had gone, but there was a stain on the tarmac, like someone had been sick.

[...] The other day I watched a grown man get punched in the face till he was basically dead, and the only thing I can't get out my mind is a baby fox that didn't do nothing but run out into the road. I keep seeing it, running, you know, on its side, but it's not the running, it's not its twisted spine, it's the eyes, Aaron, cos even though it was dying, even though its life was beaten out of it, its eyes... its eyes were on fire. **99**

Delirium

Enda Walsh

☞ **WHO**   Katerina, twenty-nine.

☞ **TO WHOM**   Ivan, twenty-six.

☞ **WHERE**   A room in Katerina's house.

☞ **WHEN**   Present day.

☞ **WHAT HAS JUST HAPPENED**   *Delirium* is based on *The Brothers Karamazov* by Dostoyevsky. It follows the story of three brothers, Mitya, Ivan and Alyosha, and their dissolute father Fyodor. Mitya is engaged to be married to Katerina but is in love with his father's whore Grushenka. Ivan meanwhile is besotted by Katerina, but his feelings are not reciprocated. Here, Katerina explains to Ivan that, even if Mitya breaks off their engagement to be with Grushenka, she will continue to adore him.

☞ **WHAT TO CONSIDER**

- The heightened realism. The style of the play could be described as Expressionistic. The monologue is darkly comic. You can be bold therefore in your playing.

- The play's theatricality. Its use of multimedia, dance, song and puppetry.

- Katerina has confused being in pain with being in love. Although the speech is comic, we are reminded of something very real and tragic about the way some women allow themselves to be abused.

☞ **WHAT SHE WANTS**

- To find a purpose to her suffering and to exalt in it.

- To find the words that best describe her experience.

- To feel alive.

☞ **KEYWORDS**   (*there are many*) gathering   direction   steer honour   duty   follow   religion   quest   devotion   charge vocation   purpose

Katerina

❝ Ivan. I've been trying to pull together the bits of me that have been lied to, been used, been betrayed. Tried to bundle up emotions that feel shredded, stamped on… It's impossible for me to fully understand the extent of my suffering, but it exists and it needs gathering… it needs… 'direction', I call it. So I thought it was important to find some words that would steer me into and through this new direction. And the words that burned into me… that… in even saying these… and they are terribly old words, Ivan… but with these two words I can see a purpose to me… the words I see are 'honour' and 'duty'. (*Slight pause.*) Honour this man. Never abandon this man. Even if this man hates me, betrays me, I will follow him always. And he may tell me to leave and I will leave but I will watch over this man all my life. And when he needs a friend, a sister, I will come to him and be his sister. This is my religion, my quest. He is my devotion. (*Slight pause.*) And even if… and I feel he may well do, Ivan… even if Mitya breaks our engagement and follows this bitch, Grushenka… honour and duty will guide me through any heartache, I'm sure of it. There is no heartache for me. Mitya is my charge, my vocation, my purpose. My whole life I will be a machine for his happiness. I will… […] I'm not explaining myself properly! You may think that I'm clinging on, that I still have hope, that I will only live if I feel that I am saving mine and Mitya's romance. I mustn't think about that now. I can't think about that any more! I'm not thinking about that impossibly slim chance! So listen again. […] I will be the ground he walks on. I will be the steps he climbs, the door he opens, the hallway he enters, the banister he places his hand on. I will be the shirt he takes off, the rug the shirt has fallen on. I will be the bed he lies on, the sheets that cover his back, the pillow his hand clenches in ecstasy, his toilet, the tissue paper he wipes himself with. The air Mitya breathes, the air that dries his brow. I am the ruffled bed he returns to from the bathroom. His darkness as he lies back beside Grushenka. A darkness that soothes his soul, that calms his breath, that finds him peace, that gives him sleep… ❞

Eight

Ella Hickson

☞ **WHO**   Astrid, early twenties.

☞ **TO WHOM**   The audience (see note on 'Direct audience address' in the introduction).

☞ **WHERE**   Her and her partner's bedroom. Her partner is asleep in the bed.

☞ **WHEN**   Present day.

☞ **WHAT HAS JUST HAPPENED**   The speech is the beginning of a longer monologue in which Astrid contemplates the causes and ramifications of infidelity. She has just returned home after a night out, having slept with another man.

☞ **WHAT TO CONSIDER**

- This is one of eight monologues that together form a full-length play.

- As with the other characters in the series, Astrid has grown up in a culture that is primarily materialistic. As Ella Hickson writes in her introduction to the play, 'a world in which the central value system is based on an ethic of commercial, aesthetic and sexual excess'.

- Astrid is described as 'slim and attractive, the kind of girl that seems comfortable in her own skin'.

- She is a little drunk.

☞ **WHAT SHE WANTS**

- To rejoice in her situation.

- To bask in the thrill of the moment.

- To savour having been wanted and desired.

- To justify her actions and to explain her lack of regret.

- To punish her partner for having ignored her.

☞ **KEYWORDS**   power   thrill   traitor   saliva   enjoy
invisible

☞ **NB**   This play offers a number of other speeches from
which to choose.

Astrid

❝ People talk about guilt as if it's an instinct. That the
second you do something wrong, you feel guilty. I don't; what
I'm feeling is power. You always join the story at the bit where
they're sorry, when they're desperately begging for
forgiveness; but there's something before that, there's now. In
the space after the act and before the consequences, when
you've got away with it; when you're walking out of an
unknown door, back down unknown streets and it's still
thumping in you – dawn's breaking, dew's settling and you're
skipping back home, flying on the thrill of it, you can taste it.
Even back here, the quiet click of the door, the tiptoe in – the
alcohol's wearing off too quickly, I want it back – our bed and
all the stuff that makes up life, our life – and – I don't feel like
a traitor; I can lie here whilst another man's saliva dries off my
lips and I can remember another man's face bearing over me –
and I enjoy it, I enjoy that all this seems new again.

His alarm's going off in ten minutes. He'll roll over and grunt,
curl himself round me like a monkey with its bloody mum.
Just like every morning. He won't notice that anything's
different – he won't see that I have mascara down my face or
that my hair is wet, because I've been running in the rain to
get back before he wakes up, he won't notice that I haven't
been here, that I'm drunk, no – for him, I became invisible a
long time ago. ❞

Fair

Joy Wilkinson

☞ **WHO**   Melanie, twenty-one, middle class, from a town in Lancashire.

☞ **TO WHOM**   Her reflection in the river.

☞ **WHERE**   The river by the fairground in a Lancashire town.

☞ **WHEN**   Around the time the play was produced in 2005. There are references to 'the war', which we take to be the war in Iraq, and to race riots reminiscent of those in Burnley in 2001.

☞ **WHAT HAS JUST HAPPENED**   At the very start of the play Melanie meets Railton (a twenty-two-year-old working-class lad from the same town in Lancashire) upside down on the Revolution ride at the fair. She goes back to his house, where they get stoned and, it is suggested, have sex. Later the same night, Railton is visited by the ghost of his father. Railton tells him about Melanie. His father is unimpressed and warns him: 'Don't you go getting distracted, you've got stuff to do. Important stuff.' In the morning, Melanie leaves without waking Railton, who has no idea where she has gone or how to contact her. Melanie, who has been to university in London and has recently returned from a trip to India and Tibet (where she was dumped by her boyfriend), is working as a community liaison officer. She is involved in a project to produce a multicultural fair that will celebrate the town's diversity one year on from local race riots. As she is about to chair a community meeting, Railton enters. She has not seen him since that night and is shocked to discover that he has come to the hall to represent a group called FAIR. 'Fighting Anti-White Racism'. It is an offshoot of the BNP, and its members are regarded by many as racist thugs. Railton's father, who died following an attack on his property by a gang of Asians, was a well-known campaigner. Melanie is disgusted and wants nothing to do with Railton. Later, when she suspects she might be pregnant by her ex-boyfriend, who is Asian, she buys a pregnancy test from the local chemist. Here in this monologue she has gone to the river. She is clutching the test in her fist and is staring at her reflection.

☞ **WHAT TO CONSIDER**

- The pregnancy test is positive. In the penultimate scene of the play Melanie is revealed in a hospital cubicle changing into her clothes under a hospital gown. We assume she has had an abortion.

- The 'we' to which she refers is her and her ex-boyfriend. Decide to what extent she is talking to him and then back to herself.

- Might she have been 'hated' so much because she was a white woman accompanied by an Asian man? It may be argued that in parts of India, as in certain parts of Britain, mixed-race couples are regarded with suspicion.

- Melanie gains a first-class honours degree, she is a vegetarian and has left-wing leanings.

- She finds it difficult to communicate with her father, who is the Principal at the local college and a Tory.

- The social and political background. Familiarise yourself with the racial tensions as experienced by the communities of towns such as Burnley and Oldham.

☞ **WHAT SHE WANTS**

- To understand her restlessness and to figure out what it is she wants.

- To find a sense of belonging.

- To figure out how and when she fell pregnant. Note how in the final sentence she uses humour to cope with the magnitude of her situation.

☞ **KEYWORDS**   healed   saved   sick   beggars   grabbing staring   hated   homesick   crap   shits

57

Melanie

❝ We went to the Kumbh Fair in Varanasi, this massive festival where millions of Hindus go to bathe in the Ganges. Lepers go to get healed, pilgrims go to get saved, I went to get… I don't know. I didn't know what I wanted to do since uni and we weren't getting on. The trip was supposed to sort all that out, but it was making things worse. Everywhere we went did my head in. It all looked so beautiful to start with, but once you'd been there a day or two it didn't look so nice any more. There were so many sick people, beggars, poor little kids, grabbing my skirt, my bag, men staring at me. I felt like they hated me for being there, for being, I don't know. For being… me. I wasn't me. It didn't seem real. It was like I wasn't really there. I felt homesick. I don't know where for. I kept thinking I'd be alright in the next place, and the next and the next, but we never got there. Then we got to Varanasi and I thought, this is it. Something real will happen to me here. And it really fucking did. The river was full of crap from factories and it gave me the shits for weeks. **❞**

Fast Labour

Steve Waters

☞ **WHO**   Anita, mid-twenties, Scottish.

☞ **TO WHOM**   Victor (her lover), Andrius and Alexei, all of whom are migrant workers from Eastern Europe.

☞ **WHERE**   The living room of a house in King's Lynn, Norfolk.

☞ **WHEN**   Present day.

☞ **WHAT HAS JUST HAPPENED**   Anita met Victor at a fish-processing factory in Scotland where he was working illegally, along with Andrius and Alexei. She was in charge of Human Resources. Some months later, Anita decides to quit her job and, on the evening before she hands in her notice, she invites Victor back to her flat where they sleep together. However, he leaves early the next morning without any word. Unbeknownst to Anita, Grimmer, an Englishman and one of the gang masters who organises these rings of workers, moves the three men on to Norfolk where they take up work as farm labourers. As time goes by, Victor (who ran a sausage factory in his native Ukraine) realises that he could be doing exactly what Grimmer does and, although it is illegal, goes about setting up a 'recruitment agency' that places migrant workers in casual labour. With a very strong Eastern European accent he feels he is likely to scare off any potential business, and so he contacts Anita, whom he persuades to work for him, in the hope that she will give the business a legitimate front. They become lovers again. Andrius is concerned that Victor has not been altogether honest with Anita ('She any idea how fifty Ukranian students end up on a ship of the line bound for Felixstowe?'), and that, when she finds out about the full extent of their illegal practices and that Victor is married with two daughters, she will betray them. Here in this speech Anita tells the men that she knows exactly what is going on.

☞ WHAT TO CONSIDER

- Anita is in love with Victor.

- At this point she is still ignorant about his wife and daughters. So far he has kept that from her. Read the play to find out what happens when she meets his wife.

- Anita is a trusting and honest person. Decide to what extent her love for Victor has coloured her judgement.

- The play centres around the exploitation of the vulnerable and the needy. The men feel as though they have sold a part of themselves. To what extent does Anita feel equally used, by a man who has never been entirely straight with her?

- The death of her mother from breast cancer at an early age and her father's ill health serve to compound her loneliness.

☞ WHAT SHE WANTS

- To assert herself.

- To show that she's no fool.

- To warn them.

☞ KEYWORDS   (*note how they are either wholesome or unwholesome*) respectable   law-abiding   dole-dodging   liberal   carefree   trust   naive   abuse   dirty   ugly   cruel

Anita

❝ Did I ever give you my CV? Don't think so. Okay, here it is: born in a boringly respectable home. Dad on the boats, on the rigs, now he's on incapacity benefit. Mum, a cleaner, paid cash in hand, died of breast cancer. Law-abiding, dole-dodging, ordinary people. Got my GCSEs and my Highers, did an extension course in Management which was bollocks, never been further afield than Portugal. That's me. Hardly worldly-wise. But no fool neither.

I know we're taking a liberal approach to the law here; I know our workers don't swan in on Eurostar, don't breeze through customs with a carefree smile; I know most of the money we make'll not pass through the hands of Inland Revenue. And I can't even believe I am saying this, even as I say it: I know what's going on.

And maybe I am mad, but I trust you to do this the way it has to be done, right. 'Cos I know for a fact it'll happen whether we do it or not and I guess I'm naive enough to believe you care more, 'cos you know more, 'cos you've been where these guys have been. And if we can do this better, cleaner and get a roof over our heads and have a wee laugh along the way, you know, I am totally utterly with you.

But if you abuse my trust – if you make this something dirty, something ugly, something cruel – I will walk out and I will not look back. Yeah?

So stick me on your letterhead, your website, your whatever. 'Cos the real question isn't, 'What do I know?', but, 'What does Grimmer know?' **99**

Gilt

Stephen Greenhorn, Rona Munro and Isabel Wright

☞ **WHO**   Jo, a teenager, Scottish.

☞ **TO WHOM**   We can assume from her last line: 'Eh… how much did you say I'd get for this?', that she is talking to a journalist.

☞ **WHERE**   Unspecified. Perhaps a café, an office of a newspaper building, or Jo's own home – you decide.

☞ **WHEN**   Present day.

☞ **WHAT HAS JUST HAPPENED**   Jo met Mick, a well-known TV presenter in his late forties, in a nightclub. She had no idea at the time who he was and only finds out when he takes her back to his hotel. While there he plies her with booze and drugs, and they end up sleeping together. When Jo phones Mick to arrange another meeting, he is convinced that she intends to blackmail him: 'TV star in underage drug orgy,' as he puts it. But Jo has actually fallen for Mick and is disappointed at his reaction. However, when he gives her a bag of fifty thousand pounds in used banknotes in order to be rid of her, she accepts the money. She is poor and living in squalor. This amount is a fortune to her. What she doesn't know, however, is that at the bottom of the bag is a note from Mick explaining that all the money is stolen and that as soon as she starts to spend it the police will be on to her. The note also says that if she wants to meet with him, he will exchange it for legal tender as long as she agrees to do anything he wants to her. But she never finds out because, having booked into a room in the same hotel where Mick is staying, a fire breaks out and all the money is destroyed. Mick also dies in the blaze. Jo's speech comes at the very end of the play and takes the form of an interview about Mick's death.

☞ **WHAT TO CONSIDER**

- The play follows the stories of seven people whose lives are strangely interwoven. Read it to understand fully the intricacies of its plot and themes.

- Jo is sexually precocious but innocent and naive in her understanding of things.

- She comes from a violent home and hasn't been back in over a year. She has been living with Chris, who is equally damaged and helpless.

☞ **WHAT SHE WANTS**

- To better herself.

- To show that she is not just a child.

- Attention.

- Money. Decide how cynical you think Jo is being or whether she believes in all that she is saying.

☞ **KEYWORDS**   shame   gutted   different   imagination   really   like   slag

Jo

❝ I think it's a shame. I was gutted when I heard. I mean, I've been wi older men before but he was different. He was really old. Thing was though he didn't treat me like a wee kid. I think he knew I had an ancient soul. So he knew he could do things as if I was a real woman, you know? And he didnae chuck me out right after. He let me hang about for a wee while. Have a fag and that. That was nice.

And he was good, you know. He wasnae quick. He was at me for fucking hours. Doing allsorts. He had a really good imagination. I like that. Don't know how I kept up but. No like I'm Ginger Spice or anything. All the yoga n' that. I was completely fucked. I think it was only the charlie that kept me going.

That was another thing. He was really generous. I mean *really* generous. He let me have as much as a wanted. Didnae bother him. He had *loads*. No shite either. Really good stuff. He said it was to do wi his job but I wasnae really listening.

See I never knew who he was. I think he liked that. That's what he said anyway. Said it gave us something in common.

Yeah. Would've been nice to see him again but I think he was dead busy. And now he's just... well...

That's how I wanted to say. So folk would know what he was like. What he was really like. So they wouldnae just slag him off.

I really, really liked him.

Pause.

Eh... how much did you say I'd get for this? 🥚🥚

Girls and Dolls

Lisa McGee

☞ **WHO**   Emma, Northern Irish, Catholic, thirties in the play (but given that she is talking about herself as a child, she could be played by a younger actress).

☞ **TO WHOM**   The audience (see note on 'Direct audience address' in the introduction).

☞ **WHERE**   'The railings' at the bottom of the street where Emma lived as a child.

☞ **WHEN**   Present day, but recalling an incident that took place in the summer of 1980.

☞ **WHAT HAS JUST HAPPENED**   The play centres on the childhood friendship of Emma and Clare, who meet in the summer of 1980. It is the school holidays, and we follow their various escapades, from shoplifting to tree-house making. Then, when a young woman, Dervla, and her baby daughter, Shannon, move in across the street from Clare, the girls offer to babysit. But Clare soon becomes obsessed with Dervla and is distressed when she sees a strange man knocking on Dervla's door. Clare's mother then goes away for a week, leaving Clare alone with her father. Although it is never shown, there is the strong suggestion that Clare is sexually abused by him. This goes part way to explaining why, at the very end of the play, she kills baby Shannon.

☞ **WHAT TO CONSIDER**

- The play is intended for two actors, who play both their older and younger selves as well as a host of other characters who make up the local community.

- The play is set in Northern Ireland at the height of 'The Troubles'.

- The speech has a subtlety and a poignancy that will be much enhanced by your reading of the play. For example, Emma's use of the expression 'Our lady wept a lot that week' and the significance of 'She was wearing two different socks' and 'Do you think they'll fly over the rainbow?' will all be made clearer.

- Arguably, not a lot happens in the speech, but it remains an opportunity for the actor to show a depth of feeling and a level of sensitivity that such delicate writing demands. You may like to 'personalise' the character of Clare, so that she becomes very real to you. Have you had a similar friendship?

☞ **WHAT SHE WANTS**

a) *As an adult with hindsight:*

- To make sense of her friend's behaviour. Decide to what extent Emma regards this incident as the first indication of Clare's troubled state of mind.

- To explain (although we the audience don't know it yet) how Clare could have done what she did.

b) *As a child in the moment:*

- To comfort and to cajole her friend.

☞ **KEYWORDS**   wept   miserable   pissing   rain   ash   smoke

☞ **NB**   This play offers a number of other speeches from which to choose.

Emma

❝ Our lady wept a lot that week. The week her mother left, it was a miserable one. Pissing with rain but still hot. I didn't see much of Clare at all, I don't think she was allowed out, you know, because of the rain. Then I was up tidying my room – well, you know, pushing things into my cupboard – and I stopped to look out the window. There she was. Sitting on the railings at the bottom of the street, on her own, just sitting there. She was wearing two different socks, it was obvious they were different as well, one was red and the other was yellow. I went out to her, I had my father's coat with me and I held it over both our heads. I didn't ask her why she was out in the rain, I didn't ask her why she had no coat on, or why she was wearing two different socks. I just started talking, I told her about my Aunt Rita, saying she had this great surprise for me, which turned out to be a statue of the Virgin Mary that glows in the dark. About me bouncing on my bed, breaking three springs, and trying to hide the evidence. Sometimes she'd smile or nod, sometimes she would laugh or say 'Really?' but I don't know if she was listening. So when I'd ran out of things to tell her, I just sat there, swinging my legs, beside her, on the railings, in the rain. Then I saw what she'd been looking at, on the telephone wires, above the street – rows and rows of birds who'd been sitting to attention, were beginning to fly away and her eyes were following them. She watched them moving off into the distance, and I turned to her and said, 'Do you think they'll fly over the rainbow?' And she said, 'No, they're not bluebirds.' But she never took her eyes off them, then she stood up, she stood up and quietly, almost under her breath said, 'You know, from here, they look just like tiny little pieces of ash, and the sky, the sky looks like smoke.' **99**

Herding Cats

Lucinda Coxon

☞ **WHO**   Justine, young professional, late twenties.

☞ **TO WHOM**   Michael, her flatmate, late twenties.

☞ **WHERE**   Sitting room, Justine's flat.

☞ **WHEN**   Present day.

☞ **WHAT HAS JUST HAPPENED**   Justine has arrived back earlier than expected after a drinking session in a pub close to where she works. She has set the alarm off and interrupted Michael, who works for a telephone sex line posing as a teenage girl. Throughout the course of the play Justine has been resisting the advances of her boss, Nigel, a much older, married man. But once she starts to succumb and thinks she may be falling in love with him, it becomes apparent that she is not the only one he has been toying with. Nigel has designs on Alexandra, the new girl. Justine feels duped and humiliated. She loses her cool, and, as she explains to Michael, instead of doing the sensible thing and returning home, she goes to the pub. Back at the flat she feels terrible. She has disturbed Michael, who was on the phone to one of his clients. He is very patient with her, clears up where she has been sick and asks her if she wants to talk about it. She does.

☞ WHAT TO CONSIDER

- Justine is single and in her late twenties. If you decide she is twenty-nine, how might it feel to be approaching thirty, with no prospect of marriage or children?

- She describes herself as sad, angry, lonely and disappointed.

- The exact job she does is unspecified. We assume that it is something to do with project-managing. Make a decision about this and decide on the nature of the company for which she works.

- Justine uses alcohol to escape the pressures of work and to blot out her feelings of unhappiness.

- What might be the emotional cost of pursuing a career and living an independent life in the city?

- Her flatmate Michael is emotionally damaged and equally unable to find intimacy.

☞ WHAT SHE WANTS

- For Michael to reassure her that she is normal. That her behaviour has been perfectly understandable and even reasonable given the circumstances. That she is not going mad.

- To relieve her feelings of terror and abject loneliness. Notice how Justine needs to talk, to have Michael listen and hold her both physically and emotionally.

☞ KEYWORDS   lost   stupid   cry   horrible   tired   dark

Justine

❝ 'You're looking very svelte'. He said. […] Svelte. As if everything was completely normal. […] I said: 'Yes I know, it's this alcohol–only diet. It's fantastic. I've only been on it a fortnight and I've already lost three days.' […] Am I stupid? […] I must be. […] Why did I want him? […] I don't even know who he is. […] He took her to lunch. 'It's Alexandra's first day… I'm taking her down to the Thai place,' he said. I said fine. 'She was a big help out in Hamburg,' he said. 'She speaks the language, her mother's Swiss. She speaks Italian too. It's a huge advantage in life having languages,' he said. 'Do you speak another language, Justine?'

I said French. Bad schoolgirl French.

And I thought he might have the balls to make a joke about bad schoolgirls. But he didn't.

I went to the pub. I wanted a drink. There was a leaving do on. Not someone I really know, but the same building. The graphics place up on the top floor, y'know. There was a woman there. She was nice to me.

It made me cry.

The emotion resurfaces for a moment. JUSTINE *fights to collect herself.*

I went back to work.

I was in his office, I was looking around.

The scene fills her head. […]

There's nothing personal. He's like the man who wasn't there. I was thinking – it's as if he doesn't exist. It's as if I just made him up. What was I thinking? […] I didn't hear him come in. He looked surprised. He said: 'Are you alright, Justine? Have you lost something?'

I said: 'What do you mean, Nigel.' I mean, I knew what he meant but what could I say… I was going through his drawers, y'know? […] 'Have you lost something?'

'No.' I said.

And he just looked at me.

'Look, Nigel… about Alexandra,' I said…

He said: 'I think she'll be an asset on the project.' I said: 'Oh, come off it – we all know you're fucking her!'

He said: 'I beg your pardon?' […]

I said: 'Christ, Nigel, she's twenty-two and she can't spell "Wednesday", why else would you ever have given her a job?' I said: 'She's twenty-two – your daughter's eighteen! What's the fuck's the matter with you? It's just horrible!'

He said: 'I think you had better go home. Go home and cool off.'

She rests in the horror of it for a moment.

I should have come straight home.

Mary Kane saw me on the way out. She said: 'You look ropey.' I said: 'I don't want to talk about it.' She said: 'I saw this coming.'

I went back to the pub. The woman had gone. I stayed a bit anyway. Stayed quite a while.

She struggles to piece together the rest.

I got a cab home, I think. I know I did. The driver wanted to talk. I can't remember what about. […]

Sometimes I don't know what I do all day. Michael. I get home and I'm so tired. It's dark when I go out, it's dark when I get home… and I'm so tired. […] 'Have you lost something…?' […] Sometimes I feel like I'm holding it all up, all on my own. […] I'm so lonely. […] And I'm so angry. […] And I feel very young sometimes. Like I haven't got a clue. And I feel… […] Sad. No, not sad. Worse than sad… I feel… […] Disappointed. **99**

The Heresy of Love

Helen Edmundson

☞ **WHO**   Sister Juana Inés de la Cruz, a Hieronymite nun in the Convent of San Jerónimo, Mexico.

☞ **TO WHOM**   Archbishop Aguiar Y Seijas.

☞ **WHERE**   The locutory of the Convent.

☞ **WHEN**   The seventeenth century.

☞ **WHAT HAS JUST HAPPENED**   Sister Juana is a much-loved and respected writer and thinker. The Court hold her in great esteem, and the Church is tolerant of her outspokenness. But with the arrival of the new Archbishop, all this changes. He has reactionary views and orders Juana to stop her writing and cease all connection to the Court. Furthermore, her once-ally Bishop Santa Cruz, wrongly believing her to have slandered him, has betrayed her by publishing her otherwise private views on the Archbishop's sermons. The Archbishop wants her tried before a private inquisition for her subversion, but he is prepared to make a deal with her. If she agrees to give up her intellectual pursuits and dedicate her life 'to prayer and simple acts of charity', he will spare her. The speech that follows is her response to him.

☞ **WHAT TO CONSIDER**

- Sister Juana was a real woman, the play is based on historical fact. Imagine, then, the extraordinary courage of this woman at a time in history when women were for the most part regarded as wholly inferior to men.

- Consider too the society that was happy to see a woman's work published and performed. Before the new Archbishop was appointed, the Church and Court were closely allied, and Juana was very much in favour.

- Juana is intellectually passionate. Watch that your emotions do not run away with you, keep connected to the thoughts she expresses. However fervent, excited and emotional she becomes, she remains clear in her thinking.

☞ **WHAT SHE WANTS**

- To make clear to the Archbishop that she will not accept his terms.

- To defend her right to speak and think freely.

- To argue the need for tolerance as a way forward.

- To argue that women are equal to men.

- To defend the right of all women to have an opinion and to express that opinion openly.

- To show that she is not acting out of arrogance or vanity, but remains humble in her thoughts and deeds.

- To challenge the Archbishop. To expose his narrow-mindedness, his ignorance and his fear.

☞ **KEYWORDS**   renounce   regret   love   care   despair   devotion   progression   truth   knowledge   light   wise

Juana

❝ Your Grace?

I am Sister Juana Inés de la Cruz.

I'm told you wish to see me. […] There is something I would like to say, Your Grace. If you'll allow it?

Whilst I stand by every argument I made against your sermon of the mandate, it was never my intention to commit my thoughts to paper, nor to have them published and distributed about the city. It was never my desire to anger or humiliate you in that way. […] I wish only that you be aware of certain facts. Of what I did and did not intend. […] I am not afraid of standing trial. I will listen to your case, whatever it might be, and I will then refute it. […] I would defend my right to think and speak as I see fit. […] I will not renounce my life. I know you have condemned me for writing plays and poems for the Court, but I do not regret them. For they are tales of love, of care, of despair and of devotion too; all the things which make us what we are. And there are prelates came before you, and will come after you, I think, who see no harm in them at all.

Nor can I regret the thoughts which I expressed upon your sermon. For are not all opinions put forth to be considered and responded to? Is that not the key to our progression? And why should men reserve all right to speak and write theology? If my thoughts are as learned, as exacting as a man's, why should they not be heard? And I have heard and read some poor and crude theology from men and yet it's given credence. If my arguments are flawed, if I am not as well informed as I should be, then criticise me, yes. And I will go away and think again and learn some more, and try again to reach towards the truth. Why should our faith fear knowledge? For knowledge comes from Him. And without it we would be as animals, wading through the mud and slime. Why should that light of knowledge be less precious, less miraculous in my mind than in yours? Where in the Bible does it say that girls cannot be wise? Show me, prove to me beyond all doubt that fact, and I will then be silent. […] There is no Devil in me. Nor do I do the Devil's work. You call on devils, I suppose, for want of any answer.

Why do you not look at me? […] I think you are afraid of me. Of all my sex. Why? Because we cannot be controlled? Or perhaps it is yourself you fear. Because to look on woman is to know you are a man. A human being. With all the frailty that implies. And all those hours you spend at night denying your humanity, they melt away. And you are left exposed! 🙶

Honour

Joanna Murray-Smith

☞ **WHO**   Sophie, twenty-four, middle class, Cambridge undergraduate, daughter of Honor and George.

☞ **TO WHOM**   Claudia, twenty-eight, Cambridge graduate, journalist, her father's lover.

☞ **WHERE**   Unspecified. Perhaps in the kitchen or sitting room of Honor and George's house. Or perhaps somewhere outside, like a café or a park – you decide.

☞ **WHEN**   Present day.

☞ **WHAT HAS JUST HAPPENED**   George has left Honor after thirty-two years of marriage and has moved in with Claudia, a woman half his age and only four years older than Sophie. Sophie has contacted Claudia and has asked that she meet with her. During their exchange, Claudia describes what sex is like with Sophie's father and tells her things about her parent's relationship that she never knew.

☞ **WHAT TO CONSIDER**

- Sophie is an only child.

- She knows that she is something of a disappointment to her father.

- The break-up of her parents' marriage has left her raw and vulnerable.

- Her father is now having sex with a woman almost her own age. How will Sophie feel about that?

- Claudia is everything that Sophie isn't: articulate, confident, beautiful and adored by George.

- Claudia was at Cambridge graduating with first-class honours when Sophie had just started.

- The feelings of jealousy and envy that Sophie is experiencing.

☞ WHAT SHE WANTS

- To make sense of the confusion in her head.

- To find a way of articulating her abstract feelings. Notice how she struggles for the necessary words.

- To be heard and to be understood.

- To remind Claudia that they were once a tight-knit family.

- To reach out to Claudia (almost like a big sister) for comfort, despite being angry at her for taking her father away.

- To be like Claudia.

☞ KEYWORDS   impossibility   choking   jungle   darkness   fallen

Sophie

❝ You're so – you're so clear. You seem so clear about things. Whereas I'm – I'm so – I can never quite say what I'm – even to myself, I'm so inarticulate. (*Beat.*) Some nights I lie awake and I go over the things I've said. Confidently. The things I've said confidently and they – they fall to pieces. (*Beat.*) And where there were words there is now just – just this feeling of – of impossibility. That everything is – there's no way through it – (*Beat.*) I used to feel that way when I was very small. That same feeling. Not a childish feeling – well, maybe. As if I was choking on – as if life was coming down on me and I couldn't see my way through it. What does a child who has everything suffer from? Who could name it? I can't. I can't. (*Breaking.*) But it was a – a sort of – I used to see it in my head as jungle. Around me. Surrounding me. Some darkness growing, something – organic, alive – and the only thing that kept me – kept me – here – was the picture of Honor and of George. Silly. (*Beat.*) Because I'm old now and I shouldn't remember that any more. Lying in bed and feeling that they were there: outside the room in all their – their warmth, their – a kind of charm to them. Maybe you're right and it was – not so simple as it looked, but they gave such a strong sense of – love for each other and inside that – I felt – I felt loved. And since I've gotten older I don't feel – (*Weeping.*) I feel as if all that – all the – everything that saved me has fallen from me and you know, I'm not a child any more. No. I'm not a kid any more. But I still feel – I need – I need... (*Beat.*) I wish – I wish I was more – Like you. Like you. **99**

How Love is Spelt

Chloë Moss

☞ **WHO**   Peta, twenty, Liverpudlian.

☞ **TO WHOM**   Colin, forty-two, her boyfriend and the father of her unborn baby.

☞ **WHERE**   Peta's bedsit, London.

☞ **WHEN**   Present day.

☞ **WHAT HAS JUST HAPPENED**   Peta has run away to London for a couple of weeks in an attempt to get away from her life back in Liverpool. She gave no warning, leaving only a note for Colin by way of explanation. She is pregnant with Colin's baby and needs time and space to figure out what it is she wants. After a series of unhappy encounters she feels fearful, misses Colin and asks him to come and take her home. Before they leave, Peta is insistent that Colin listens to her. She needs to tell him things.

☞ **WHAT TO CONSIDER**

- Peta has had a troubled life and ran away from home when she was sixteen.

- Peta's mother disowned her and her father shows no interest.

- We are given to understand that Colin has rescued Peta from a life that might otherwise have been lived on the streets.

- He is twenty-two years older than her, set in his ways, and as much a father to her as a lover. He has given Peta stability, but she feels trapped by the certainty/predictability of their life together, especially now that she is pregnant.

- Peta has hurt Colin by leaving in the way that she did.

- Colin tells her that if he is to take her back she must prove to him that she is ready to commit both to him and to the baby.

- To what extent does her behaviour change from that of a girl to that of a woman and then back again? Some of her new-found insight points to an increased maturity. The play ends, however, with her drinking a glass of milk like a child. Does that suggest she will remain a little girl or does it imply that she is leaving the child behind and moving toward a new kind of womanhood? Perhaps milk is good for the unborn baby and Peta is determined to take care of it. What might this final image signify? You decide.

☞ **WHAT SHE WANTS**

- To explain to Colin that she needed to exert her independence, even if it was short-lived.

- To reassure him that while they were apart she still needed him.

- To share with him the message in neon lettering that somehow symbolises their future together.

- To close one chapter of her life in order to move on to the next.

- For Colin to take her seriously.

☞ **KEYWORDS**   Crystal   shell   cry   rubble

Peta

❝ When I first got here I spent a day… a whole day on buses. I got a Travelcard and I just got on different buses. Like we did that day. I just thought I'd see where I ended up. But it wasn't like when we did it. […] I went to Crystal Palace first. I thought… I imagined something different. Crystal Palace. I bought a fried-egg sandwich from this café… by the terminus. And it had shell in it. I wanted to cry. That made me want to cry. I felt about eight… or something. I wanted you. (*Beat.*) Then I got back on a bus and I went to Victoria and I got another bus. A 38. I just sat on it 'til I had to get off. And I got off and just walked for a bit… just walking. I turned down this road… this little road. It was just normal. Just houses, cars… but at the end of it was this sort of… it was like this Roman building like… huge columns… colonnades… a pointed-roof bit. Really gorgeous and a bit, you know… mad… because it was just there at the top of this road with houses and cars and that wasn't the part though. Along the top of it… the whole width of it was – it wasn't switched on but there were neon tubes. Lettering that said, 'Everything's going to be alright.' Just that. Everything's going to be alright. […] I went back yesterday – before I phoned yer… and it was just rubble. Thought I'd imagined it. Asked this woman cleaning the windows of her house. I asked her if it had said that and she said, 'Yeah.' I would have liked to show it to you but it isn't there any more. That's it. **"**

How to Curse

Ian McHugh

☞ **WHO**   Miranda, seventeen, from Great Yarmouth.

☞ **TO WHOM**   The audience (see note on 'Direct audience address' in the introduction), and herself.

☞ **WHERE**   Her friend Nick's bedsit on Great Yarmouth seafront.

☞ **WHEN**   Present day.

☞ **WHAT HAS JUST HAPPENED**   Miranda and Nick, both seventeen, hang out together. They are highly imaginative, love books and enjoy winding each other up with their literary arguments. Nick is obsessed with Shakespeare's *The Tempest* and he and Miranda have been collecting random items in order to conjure a storm. But there is something missing. While Nick has cast himself in the role of Prospero, he needs someone who can perform his instructions as Ariel does in *The Tempest*. Then Nick and Miranda meet William, another seventeen-year-old, who Nick believes he can groom. Here in this monologue, Miranda is practising a magic trick.

☞ **WHAT TO CONSIDER**

- Miranda's love of literature and poetry. She says she read Sylvia Plath's *The Bell Jar* five times when she was about fourteen.

- Her rebellious nature. She asks William, 'Do you ever get the urge to do purely wicked things, just for the sake of it?'

- Her father is a magician. She calls him 'a total cock'. We gather that her mother does some sort of social work. She wants to move out of her parents' home.

- She has a boyfriend called Francis, whom she met down the pub. We do not get the impression that she is in love with him.

- Her relationship with Nick, the 'he' to whom she refers in her speech, is volatile and intense. It is however platonic.

- The seafront at Great Yarmouth. The run-down nature of the town and the greyness of the North Sea. There is, however, something hugely atmospheric, even majestic about this English seaside town.

- 'Come unto these yellow sands' is a quotation from Ariel in *The Tempest.*

- Make a decision about how you will perform the magic trick (see note on using props in the introduction). It is a well-known trick and can be purchased easily and cheaply online or in joke shops.

☞ **WHAT SHE WANTS**

- To test her powers.

- A hit.

- To escape her otherwise boring life, which consists of hanging out in the precinct, at home or with Francis in the pub.

☞ **KEYWORDS** buzzing sticking itches stillness debris shifted realigned configurations spell grabs drags

Miranda

" *As she speaks she performs a magic trick: she passes a green handkerchief through her closed fist several times; on the final pass it becomes a red handkerchief.*

Haven't you ever really wanted it? On one of those nights when the flies are buzzing round your face and sticking to your skin, and the back of your neck itches and you can hardly breathe? Haven't you ever just wanted to see the sky light up and have the wind blow you sideways and the thunder press against your throat?

And what comes after. The stillness. The debris. How things have shifted and realigned. New configurations. Imbalances righted.

He had me half-convinced. I egged him on. Of course, I didn't know how to do it, and nor did he. But it has to be possible, right?

She laughs.

No, me neither. But there was something beautiful about the way he worked. He wouldn't give up. Someone must know.

It's convincing, isn't it? All these books. All those words, strung together. It's like a spell. It is a spell. It's very clever, how convincing it is. It's a whole world; it exists, real as any other world. And it grabs hold of you, it drags you in. To the point at which your own world ceases to exist.

(*As she completes the trick.*) Come unto these yellow sands.   **"**

Immaculate

Oliver Lansley

☞ **WHO**   Rebecca, twenty-/thirty-something.

☞ **TO WHOM**   Mia, her best friend.

☞ **WHERE**   The living room of Mia's flat.

☞ **WHEN**   Present day.

☞ **WHAT HAS JUST HAPPENED**   Despite splitting up from her ex-boyfriend Michael eleven and a half months ago, and despite not having had sex in all that time, Mia finds herself pregnant. It turns out that Mia has been supernaturally impregnated, but when the Archangel Gabriel and Lucifer both show up claiming parentage, nobody is sure by whom. (Hence the play's title *Immaculate* as in the Immaculate Conception.) In the meantime, her best friend Rebecca has been (secretly) going out and having sex with Michael. Neither of them has told Mia. But when Michael finds out that Mia is pregnant and tells Rebecca, she immediately assumes (wrongly) that Michael is the father and that Mia and Michael are still sleeping with each other, and that Michael is in effect cheating on them both. She arrives at Mia's flat to confront the situation.

☞ **WHAT TO CONSIDER**

- The play is a farce, and while the characters are wholly believable, the situation is fantastic.

- The punctuation. The speech is long, but there are very few full stops. Before the speech there is the stage direction 'all gabbled at an incredible rate'. Make sure, however, that the speech does not run away with you. Be aware of all the different thoughts and then the places where the thought changes. When you deliver the speech you will need to be not just speaking quickly but also thinking quickly. In this way, the speech will have variety.

☞ **WHAT SHE WANTS**

- To come clean about her relationship with Michael. Decide to what extent she needs Mia's forgiveness.

- To express her hurt that she has been lied to, and at the same time to express her shame for having lied.

- To make sense of the confusion. Decide to what extent she blames herself for the situation. Note her terror of what the future might hold.

☞ **KEYWORDS**   *(there are many, but note how often she uses the following)* didn't   couldn't   weren't   haven't   don't

Rebecca

❝ Hi… Look, there's something I have to say. I probably should have told you earlier, but I didn't know if it was going anywhere but now I think it is, or thought it was, but now you're pregnant, so I probably shouldn't tell you anyway 'cause stress is bad for the baby, not that you're keeping it, right? God, you're huge, are those my boots…?

Look… Michael and I are together…

We're a couple, I'm sorry I didn't tell you, I didn't plan it, I was out and saw Michael and said hello and we got talking and it came out that he'd always quite fancied me but couldn't do anything about it obviously 'cause we were best mates and I said I quite fancied him too, which was why I was sometimes a bit of a bitch towards him because I think subconsciously I fancied him and I always used to talk to Ed about him, and that's why Ed never wanted to come out with us in a foursome because he thought I fancied Michael which I didn't, or didn't think I did, but turns out I did, because I fancy him now, anyway, we weren't going to do anything because you two had just broken up and I knew how pissed off you'd be but then we said, well, maybe we should just have a kiss, while we're both single then, just to get it out of our systems, so we had a kiss, and then the kiss carried on, and things and things and we ended up having sex, which I'm not proud of but it was good, but it was bad because the condom broke and I had to get the morning-after pill, which was fucking awful and I was terrified 'cause I thought I was gonna have a baby, and you know how much I fucking hate babies 'cause of that dream I have with all the babies that have my mum and dad's faces who shit and piss and cry and I can't stop them! And also the pill made me feel really ill, and that was the day we were supposed to go to Bluewater to try and find some shoes to go with that brown skirt you got from Hennes and I said I couldn't come 'cause I was sick and you were pissed off and I wanted to tell you but I couldn't and I felt really guilty, and I cried, and then I called Michael and told him and he was really good about it and made me feel better, and we had decided we weren't gonna see each other again, but I was crying on the phone so he came over and then he ended up staying the night again, but we didn't have sex, we just cuddled and then it went from there.

But now you tell me that you're pregnant and you say that you haven't had sex with anyone since Michael, which means he must be the father but you don't want to tell me because I made such a fuss about what a fucker he was when he dumped you. Which means you're lying to me and he's lying to me, and I'm lying to you, and you're fucking him and I'm fucking him and he's fucking you… and me… and I'm going to lose my best friend and my boyfriend, not that I call him my boyfriend but technically he is, and I'll be helpless and hopeless and friendless and loveless and die old and alone with thread veins and bladder weakness and a houseful of cats… **"**

Invisible
Tena Štivičić

☞ **WHO**   Lara, Eastern European, twenties.

☞ **TO WHOM**   An imagined interviewer.

☞ **WHERE**   The kitchen of a well-off household where she works as a cleaner.

☞ **WHEN**   The middle of the first decade of the twenty-first century.

☞ **WHAT HAS JUST HAPPENED**   Lara is an Eastern European immigrant to London, fantasising about her future while in fact working as a cleaner. Before starting the speech, she shines a lamp directly onto her face, as if she were giving a television interview.

☞ **WHAT TO CONSIDER**

- The hardship Lara has had to endure.
- Her bravery.
- Her ambition.
- Her refusal to be beaten.

☞ **WHAT SHE WANTS**

- To assimilate into British culture.
- To maintain her dignity.
- To fantasise about her future in order to escape the pain of her present.
- To believe that her dream could become a reality.

☞ **KEYWORDS**   imagine   tough   hard   cleaner/cleaning/clean   ashamed   fine   expensive   impressed   friends

Lara

❝ Would you like a cup of tea? Milk and sugar? I take it quite strong. You know, before I came here I couldn't imagine putting milk in tea. And now I can't get enough of it. (*Pause.*) Yes, it was tough the first few years. Very tough. But even when it was very hard… you learn things every day. Every day you are a little better at… living here. I can't explain. First time I had A to Z in my hands, I wanted to cry. Then one day you just catch yourself going '5C, eighty-nine.' (*Pause as if to hear a question.*) I worked as a cleaner. I don't say that I was a cleaner, I just worked as a cleaner. I'm not ashamed of cleaning. You have to make money. I was a good cleaner because I clean houses like they were my own. And we are much more thorough with cleaning than English. Yes, I have a cleaner now. I treat her well. I'm not saying she's my best friend but I take an interest. I never behave like she is not there. (*Pause.*) Well, this is how it happened. One lady I worked for, she was going to throw out some of her clothes. I asked if I could have them. They were very fine, expensive clothes. Then I went home and I changed them to fit me. I also changed the design a bit. When she saw what I did, she was impressed. She recommended me to a friend who had a company that makes clothes. So I started to work for him and slowly, little by little, I started my own business, making clothes. It's doing very well now. Karen, that's the lady I worked for, she and I are good friends now. She even wears the clothes I make now. **❞**

it felt empty when the heart went at first but it is alright now

Lucy Kirkwood

☞ **WHO**   Dijana, Eastern European, twenty and then twenty-one, sex worker.

☞ **TO WHOM**   The audience (see note on 'Direct audience address' in the introduction), and her lost daughter.

☞ **WHERE**   A modern, sparsely decorated flat.

☞ **WHEN**   Present day.

☞ **WHAT HAS JUST HAPPENED**   The speech comes close to the beginning of the play. As the lights come up, Dijana has just killed a bird, that had flown in through an open window, with a rolled-up newspaper. We soon discover that Dijana has been working as a prostitute and that she only needs thirty more pounds to make up the twenty thousand pounds she owes her pimp Babac in order for him to give her back her passport so that she can stop working in this way. She has calculated that her next client will be her very last and that the following morning she will 'come to find you… We are going to swim in the sea… In Brighton'. It is at this point that we realise she is addressing her daughter, as if we the audience are that lost child. As she further contemplates the bird, she is reminded of something else that was strange this morning.

☞ **WHAT TO CONSIDER**

- The play follows the plight of young women who have fallen prey to sex traffickers. It was produced by Clean Break theatre company, who work with women whose lives have been affected by the criminal justice system.

- Dijana's story was inspired by real-life events.

- Kingsland Road is in the London Borough of Hackney.

☞ **WHAT SHE WANTS**

- To show that she can handle her situation, that she doesn't need help and that she is in control. To what extent is this a front? A show of bravado? Note how proud Dijana is and how she uses humour to brush off painful feelings.

- Power over the men she sleeps with or at least an understanding that she is their equal. Note how upset she becomes when her client assumes that she has not heard of Waitrose.

- To make it clear that she is not just a piece of meat. She is fully aware of the paradoxical nature of this man who, while supplying dead flesh to upmarket supermarkets, is in turn buying live flesh from the women who sell their bodies. The irony is not wasted on her.

☞ **KEYWORDS**   strange   weird   meat   supplier   pig   prick

☞ **NB**   This play offers a number of other speeches from which to choose.

Dijana

❝ [*She*] *Picks up two bottles.*

Look. Babac did not give me these I took them by myself from bootsthechemist.

L'Oréal shampoo. And conditioner too. Because I'm worth it!

She pulls her hair out of its ponytail like she's in a shampoo advert and shakes her head in slow motion.

See.

But she doesn't laugh.

This is extra funny because I know exactly how much I am worth. How many people can say this! I am worth one thousand euros because that is how much Babac pay for me.

To put this in easy language, that is like two-and-a-half iPhones.

Something strange happen this morning […] This guy, he come and we fuck. Just normal him on top once then in my mouth and he come on my tits but after he go something weird, he go

Ummm… do you want me to call someone?

And in my head I am like Yeah do you have number of a dentist cos your breath stink.

But I do not say out loud. I do not say nothing.

But this guy he is still standing there and my next client he is coming and the guy he is looking all red and English like meat and he go Ummm you don't have to do this if you don't want you know.

And in my head I'm like Uh, okay it is like none of your business! Shit! Like I don't do what I want you know? I am fine. You think I stay here if I am not fine? I am fucking great mate! And anyway it is not like there are so many things I could do you know! It is not like I went to Oxford University or something!

Anyway I tell him, Today is my last day, *actually*. That shut him up!

He go, Oh.

Yeah I say, Tomorrow I will not be working here no more, which actually is true, I say I am starting new job in an office in the Canary Wharf, which is a small lie but who give a fuck right. I say Where do *you* work? […] What is your job?

And he says I am a supplier.

And I am like Yeah. And I yawn, to show how boring he is. Of what?

And he says Pigs.

She raises her eyebrows.

Okay. And what do you supply to these pigs?

No, he say, I supply pork. I am a pork supplier.

[…]

The meat is so good he say. You should taste it. You would not believe. The difference in taste.

How much it cost I say. And he say a number and I laugh, I have a head for numbers and that is a fucking stupid price to pay for some bit of pig you can get it so cheap in Kingsland Road.

And he look sad then, and he go Our customers can afford it. Our customers believe to pay for quality.

Who your customers, I am shouting now I don't know why, What shop you sell this in!

Waitrose, he go. And then I am quiet so he say, It is a supermarket, and *that* make me MAD so I go YEAH I KNOW. And I am bored of this now and his time is over so I put my bra on and that tells him.

Good luck with your new job, he go, as he walk out.

I see he has forgot to do up his flies.

Beat.

Prick. **99**

Ladies Down Under

Amanda Whittington

☞ **WHO**   Shelley, twenty-six, from Hull.

☞ **TO WHOM**   Danny, a traveller, Australian.

☞ **WHERE**   A campsite, Uluru, Australia.

☞ **WHEN**   March 2007.

☞ **WHAT HAS JUST HAPPENED**   *Ladies Down Under* is the sequel to *Ladies' Day*, in which four fish-factory workers from Hull – Shelley, Jan, Pearl and Linda – win a small fortune at the races. One and a half years on, they have booked a holiday to Sydney, Australia. However, when Jan's boyfriend Joe fails to meet them at the airport, they decide to change their plans and head further afield. They travel to Queensland and on to Uluru where they set up camp. It is here that they are reunited with Joe and meet Danny, who has been accompanying him. Just before they leave the camp, Pearl, Linda and Jan go for a walk, leaving Shelley to start the packing up. Danny is with her. When she is then bitten by a spider and asks Danny to kill it, he attempts to show Shelley that there is nothing to fear. He tells her 'Change your thoughts, you change the world.' As he turns to go she calls back to him. The speech that follows is made up of the conversation they then have.

☞ **WHAT TO CONSIDER**

- Shelley loves all things 'bling'. However, when her luggage is lost in Singapore, she starts an inward journey of the soul and comes to realise the true value of things. Read the play to find out how her relationship with Danny develops.

- Her mother was killed by a car when Shelley was young. She had no other family and was put into foster care.

- Her dream has been to be a model.

- Her inner turmoil. A part of her is beginning to realise that the kind of lifestyle she has been pursuing is fake; however, she is not quite ready to give it all up and is unsure what to put in its place.

☞ WHAT SHE WANTS

- To get off the 'merry-go-round' she has created for herself.
- To give vent to her feelings of loss and regret.
- To rest in a moment of calm before she must return to all that is drab and depressing back home.
- To express all this out loud.
- For Danny to offer some words of wisdom. Decide to what extent her initial question to him is rhetorical or genuine.

☞ KEYWORDS   sad   miss/missed   stuck   selfish   shallow   dream

Shelley

❝ Danny? How do I change this? […] I won some money a while back. A hundred grand. Left my job. Went shopping. New kitchen, new bathroom. Got my teeth done and my tits. Now I've got shoes I'll never wear and bags I don't want. I've got a Cartier watch but I can't work the cooker. I drink and smoke and go clubbing on a Monday. I mean, how sad is that? All the men I meet are arseholes and I miss my mates at work. I'm twenty-six years old, so I've missed the modelling boat. I think I've missed the boat, full stop. I'm stuck in Hull and I've got three grand left. Three grand to pay for all this, then I'm back in the fish plant. […] It's all right. I don't want your sympathy. I just wanted to… Well, like you said, I'll not see you again. I just wanted to say it out loud. […] And I know what you're thinking. She's selfish and shallow and you're right, I am. But you've not seen where I come from, it's not lovely like this. I just want to live the dream a bit longer, that's all. ❞

Limbo*

Declan Feenan

☞ **WHO**   Girl, late teens, Northern Irish.

☞ **TO WHOM**   The audience (see note on 'Direct audience address' in the introduction).

☞ **WHERE**   The shore of a mountain lake.

☞ **WHEN**   Present day.

☞ **WHAT HAS JUST HAPPENED**   The speech that follows is the beginning of a much longer monologue. The play tells the story of the Girl's relationship with an older, married man. She has a daughter by him and he is supportive, but he cannot be with her, and in the final passage we understand that she means to drown herself. It is only then that we get the full significance of her opening line: 'I think I've always had a fear of water.'

☞ **WHAT TO CONSIDER**

- The writer has not given the Girl a name. What might this suggest to you?

- At sixteen she had already left home and was living on her own. Note how, on the day of her seventeenth birthday, she considers 'phoning home', but does not.

- Her backstory. We know very little about what has happened to the girl up until the age of seventeen. You might like to use this opportunity to create a fully rounded character for yourself and, by doing so, fill in all the gaps.

- Find different voices for when you characterise 'Shauna', 'Lizzie' and 'Estelle'.

- The feel of the crucifix around her neck. She makes a point of showing it to us.

- She will meet the older man in the nightclub where the girls are headed.

* Published in the volume *St Petersburg and Other Plays*

☞ **WHAT SHE WANTS**

- To explain how she came to this point (i.e. on the shore of the lake, about to take her own life).

- To justify her final act.

- Forgiveness.

☞ **KEYWORDS**   fear   water   lovely   surprise   soaked   peeled   velvet

☞ **NB**   This play offers a number of other speeches from which to choose.

Girl

❝ I think I've always had a fear of water.
There's something about it.
Besides being wet.
Don't get me wrong – I like water.
I drink it.
I wash with it.
But…
It was raining on the morning of my seventeenth birthday.
I went into work as usual.
John, the line manager, called me into his office.
You only get called in if you're stealing or fiddling your clock-in card.
John has the slowest voice in the world.
(*John.*) 'Youse wanna come in now?'
I felt someone behind me.
It was Shauna.
She was carrying a cake – candles and everything.
Estelle was there as well, Anne Marie and Lizzy, a whole crowd of them.
They started to sing 'Happy Birthday'.
I didn't know they knew.
The cake was one of those sponge ones you get in petrol stations.

It was lovely.

It was a complete surprise.

I'd been working with the girls for a few months – packing line in the meat factory.

The girls were older than me – mostly in their mid-twenties.

I think I was the youngest on the floor.

I remember that as a lovely day.

It would've been dull if they hadn't done that.

On the way home I missed the bus and had to walk.

I got completely soaked.

I got home and put the kettle on.

I thought about phoning home, but I didn't.

I peeled off my clothes and put them in the machine.

I showered and decided to shave my legs – why not?

I put on my dressing gown and read a magazine.

The doorbell rang.

It was the girls.

They had loads of drink.

They sat me down.

Shauna knelt down and held my hands.

(*Shauna.*) 'Right, I don't want you to say anything, but we've all had a whip-around.'

(*Lizzy.*) 'We have.'

(*Estelle.*) 'Yep.'

(*Shauna.*) 'Here, we hope you like it.'

The box was velvet.

It was a silver necklace with a cross on it.

This one here.

Shauna started pouring drinks and Estelle got to work.

(*Estelle.*) 'Right, we have to get you ready. Isn't that right, Lizzy?'

(*Lizzy.*) 'That's right. We can't have her looking like that. I'll get my bag.'

(*Estelle.*) 'We are taking you to Oak and Chrome. Top spot. You're going to love it, isn't she, Shauna?'

(*Shauna.*) 'Yep. It's just opened. It's really nice. Swanky.'

(*Estelle.*) 'Shauna knows the doorman, don't you, Shauna?'

(*Shauna.*) 'Yep. Lovely fella, really down to earth – '

(*Estelle.*) 'Shauna's shagged him – '

(*Shauna.*) 'He's a lovely fella – '

(*Estelle.*) 'What are you going to wear?'

I didn't really have anything.

(*Estelle.*) 'Is your wardrobe in your room?'

Estelle ran up the stairs and I could hear her rummaging.

She came back down.

(*Shauna.*) 'Jesus, Estelle…'

(*Estelle.*) 'Like a glove!'

(*Shauna.*) 'You can't have her wearing that.'

(*Estelle.*) 'Why not?

(*Shauna.*) 'It's lime green!'

(*Estelle.*) 'That's the point… Shauna, is there any drink on the go or what?'

We drank.

Lizzy did my hair and made me up.

Of course, Estelle and Lizzy got louder and louder and when the taxi arrived Lizzy started flirting with the driver.

She told him she'd forgotten her purse and could she pay him some other way.

He asked her what she had in mind.

She told him, 'Fuck off, you're older than my dad.' **"**

Little Baby Jesus

Arinze Kene

☞ **WHO**   Joanne, fifteen, mixed race.

☞ **TO WHOM**   The audience (see note on 'Direct audience address' in the introduction).

☞ **WHERE**   Inner-city London. Exact location is unspecified. Perhaps she is talking to us in her bedroom, a street or the park. You decide.

☞ **WHEN**   Present day.

☞ **WHAT HAS JUST HAPPENED**   The play, a series of interconnected monologues, describes the point at which three teenagers, Joanne, Kehinde and Rugrat, begin to grow up. They speak directly to the audience. At this point in the play we know that Joanne lives with her mother in a council house. She and her mother, who suffers from depression, do not get on. She has a half-brother to whom she does not speak. When she is not at school she works in a launderette. She has kissed Rugrat, but then meets a boy called Baker. (Later on in the play she will fall in love with Kehinde.) When her mother is sectioned, Joanne is sent to the north of England to stay in a foster retreat. In the speech that follows, she describes what it is like there.

☞ **WHAT TO CONSIDER**

- Her mother's depression, and the impact it has on her everyday life.

- At school Joanne is known as Jodie. Rugrat tells us how 'Joanne' is nice, and how 'Jodie' is evil and rude.

- To what extent does the persona of 'Jodie' allow Joanne to cope in the world?

- The pace and stress of inner-city London life.

- Being in the countryside enables Joanne to take a step back and to take stock.

- Later we will discover that Joanne is pregnant with Baker's child.

- Read the play to find out what happens to the baby.

☞ WHAT SHE WANTS

- To feel normal. Being with other people of her own age, some of whom are even more disturbed, allows her that.

- To feel safe.

- Company. Although she describes the retreat as a 'mad house', it allows her a break from the loneliness of living with her mother and her mother's depression.

☞ KEYWORDS   crustified/crust   flopped   enjoy

☞ NB   This play offers a number of other speeches from which to choose.

Joanna

❝ I dunno… the retreat was… alright. But everyone was younger than me, which was kinda disappointing – having no one your age there to chat to.

It looked NOTHING like the flyer. Them dere people who made the flyer are jokers – real talk. I gets there now, all the colours had faded on the building. The children there were looking crustified, dear Lord; crust! I thought I had it bad. One of them looked like she was wearing a potato sack. Another one look like he stole his clothes off of a scarecrow. Caveman couture as well; no shoes. Some people do not have it. It's a sad world, man.

On the first day you could tell who and who were gonna clash. It was like the Big Brother House for Teenage Rejects and Unwanted Infants. Some dramatic kids up in there, boy. Crying like it was first day of school. Little Jack was crying like he sold his cow for some beans and never got the beanstalk – real talk. I told everyone straight –

'Oi oi, listen! I'm the oldest here, innit. So like… yeah… just… just have respect and dat… For me.'

Ah, I flopped it, innit. Like George Bush, I had everyone's attention and flopped severely. You know when you tell everyone to stop, and then everyone actually stops dead like, and they're all just looking at you, and that kinda surprises you because you never thought they would pay you any mind, so you forget what you was gonna say? Real Talk.

(*Mocking herself.*) '*…just have respect for me and dat.*'

We were *all* fucked up in that place anyhow so I blended in nicely with that intro.

There was this girl, Frankie. I think Frankie's a crack-baby, the most hyperest thirteen-year-old in the world. She already had this raspy voice and she was always screaming and shouting and talking (bitching) and laughing or whistling that loud whistle, the one where you jam up two fingers in your mouth – I hate when people do that indoors. Why? I beg, it's not necessary –

'*Okay Frankie, we all know you can do it now, stop showing off –*
REAL!'

And boy was she oversexed. Always chatting wet 'bout some boy who was banging her doggy-style under some bridge after dark. Then I'll overhear her telling someone else the same story but she'd say it was on *top* of the bridge before sunset. Lying through her muddy braces. A mad house. But I actually started to enjoy myself… **99**

Little Dolls*

Nancy Harris

☞ **WHO**   Vicky, late twenties, from a privileged background.

☞ **TO WHOM**   John, her therapist.

☞ **WHERE**   A room without light.

☞ **WHEN**   Present day.

☞ **WHAT HAS JUST HAPPENED**   This speech comes at the start of the play. During a session with her therapist, Vicky is attempting to recall a traumatic incident from her childhood when she went on a school trip to the Continent.

☞ **WHAT TO CONSIDER**

- Although, at this point in the play, we the audience don't know where her story is heading, John the therapist has heard it before, and there is an underlying tension as she talks about Denise in the past tense – 'she had lovely black hair… I'm sure you've seen the pictures' – and menace in the way she explains, 'I can understand why the Madame said she never thought to lock the doors.' We later discover that Denise was murdered by an intruder as she and the other girls slept. Decide to what extent Vicky feels guilty about the fact that she did not wake up and was therefore unable to help her best friend.

- Vicky is suffering from a kind of post-traumatic stress syndrome. She is acutely anxious and is unable to lead what she describes as a 'normal' life.

- She is terrified of the dark. Her session takes place in a room without light in order to cure her of her phobia.

- The play happens in real time, meaning it is as long as the therapy session it depicts.

- Make sure you have a very strong sense of all that Vicky describes. Because the speech is about an event from the past

* Published in the volume *Our New Girl*

and is so descriptive, it is vital that you provide clear images for yourself.

☞ **WHAT SHE WANTS**

- To free herself from the torment of that night. She is prompted by her therapist to recall it, but she can only get so far until she has to stop. Decide to what extent she wants to please her therapist as much as she wants to heal herself.

- To lead a normal life with a job and a boyfriend.

- To feel safe.

☞ **KEYWORDS** *(note how they are either something nice or menacing)* friendly dark tired pretty sweets cake giggle nerves cranky heavy cosy

☞ **NB** This play offers a number of other speeches from which to choose.

Vicky

❝ Where was I? Oh.

Well, I – suppose we got to the hostel some time after eleven. We had left Paris early that evening and had been driving for three maybe, four hours in the dark. We were tired. We had started the journey singing, but – we weren't singing by the time we arrived. The hostel was pretty. Lots of wood and watercolours on the walls. A friendly overweight woman had been waiting up for us – Madame… something. We could hear the sound of crickets or frogs in the distance all around – Denise was mimicking them but Mrs Lynch told her to stop. It was getting on her nerves. Everyone was cranky with the heat. We each got a glass of orange and a biscuit and then were sent to bed because of the early start. They split us into groups of two, six in each room. I took the bed beside Denise, of course.

Normally, we would've stayed up. Past curfew, you know. Talking. Or – or eating sweets, or little cakes that we, that we would've bought when Mrs Lynch or one of the other's backs were turned and we would've giggled I guess. Little girls giggle. But that night we were so – after all the travelling. I didn't brush my teeth. Denise did. And her hair. She – um – she had lovely black hair. Thick and straight. I'm sure – I'm sure you've seen the pictures. Everybody comments.

She brushed it a hundred times before going to bed at night. Every night. Imagine. I – well – I thought that was great. I don't think she managed one hundred that night but she – did as many as she could. And then. Well, then we went to bed. In our little white nighties. I don't think we even said goodnight. Our eyes were that heavy. Denise had her back to me. I could see the outline of her shoulders underneath the sheets and we just – drifted off. You see it was that sort of place, the hostel. It felt – cosy.

I can understand why the Madame said she never thought to lock the doors. **99**

Little Gem

Elaine Murphy

☞ **WHO**   Amber, eighteen, Dubliner.

☞ **TO WHOM**   The audience (see note on 'Direct audience address' in the introduction).

☞ **WHERE**   In a cubicle of the toilets at the call centre where she works, and then at her desk in the call centre.

☞ **WHEN**   Present day.

☞ **WHAT HAS JUST HAPPENED**   Amber, recently out of school, and besotted with her new boyfriend Paul, has been enjoying regular nights on the town. Last night she was drinking vodka, smoking spliffs with Paul and his friends, and did 'a line of coke' with her best friend Jo. She was upset because Paul had been flirting with other women and keeps talking about wanting to go to Australia (without her). Amber's friend Jo says that, until someone else comes along, Amber is just a 'handy hole' for Paul. Nevertheless she spends the night with Paul, and when she wakes up in the morning she feels terrible and is sick in Paul's bathroom. Ordinarily, she would 'pull a sicky' and not go in to work, but it was Jo's father who got her the job and she feels a sense of loyalty. Once at work she feels ill again and rushes to the toilets where she meets Mandy from the accounts department. Mandy 'jokes' with her saying that she 'hope's it's not morning sickness'. Amber, worried by this, asks Jo to cover for her while she goes to the chemist to buy a pregnancy test. The speech starts with her sitting on the toilet waiting for the result.

☞ **WHAT TO CONSIDER**

- The play is a series of interwoven monologues telling the story of a year in the life of Amber, her mother Lorraine and her grandmother Kay.

- Amber is an only child.

- Her father is a drug addict and no longer lives with the family. He stole to feed his habit, and when Amber was younger he stole her confirmation money. To what extent has her relationship with her father affected her ability to form intimate and trusting relationships with men? Note how Amber has chosen a boyfriend who is afraid of commitment and note how jealous she becomes when he talks to other women.

- Her relationship with her mother is fraught. Lorraine is taking medication for depression and neither woman feels they can open up to each other.

- Amber is closer to her grandmother than to her mother. When she finds out she is pregnant she tells her grandmother first.

- Is her appetite for drink and drugs that of a regular eighteen-year-old recently out of school (and part of a general culture of binge-drinking and partying)? Or does it suggest to you that Amber is an emotionally damaged character and is using drugs and alcohol as a way of escaping painful experiences?

- To what extent does she use humour and bravado as a way of dealing with her problems and masking her vulnerability?

- How might it feel to be pregnant by someone who doesn't love you? And in circumstances that are far from romantic?

☞ WHAT SHE WANTS

- To find out whether she is pregnant. Decide to what extent she would secretly like this. 'If I was… Paul'd have to…' Despite her fears, perhaps she hopes that being pregnant will bring her and Paul closer together.

- To figure out when the conception took place.

- To come to terms with what has happened.

☞ KEYWORDS   pregnant   ma   da   yokes   necrophilia baby

☞ NB   This play offers a number of other speeches from which to choose.

Amber

❝ In two minutes I'll get an 'accurate' reading. Imagine me being pregnant? Like, a ma. There's no way. Imagine Paul being a da! That's mad. Like, I know I've nothing to worry about but Mandy has my head doing fucking overtime. My yokes are always all over the place but… I actually can't remember when I got my last one. If I was… Paul'd have to… (*Looks at the strip.*) Oh my God, my heart. Negative. I knew it. Open the door; show Jo. The fucking relief. I knew it, but you know… Jo checks the box, then checks it again. She says it's positive. Give over, an 'X' means no. She turns it a bit and says: 'Plus means positive.' Bollix.

Sitting at my desk waiting for calls to come through. I'm on directory enquiries today for an English phone company. This fella rings in, looking for a cab firm in Hackney. He doesn't know the name of the place or the road it's on but it's definitely somewhere in Hackney, yeah… Do I not know it? How would I bleedin' know it? I'm about to start a search, but it feels too much like work and he's been real ignorant so I cut him off. Trying to remember when the fuck it could've happened cos in fairness we're always real careful. I've done three pregnancy tests and they all say the same thing.

There was this one night, when we got back to his gaff and I was wrecked. Was lying there waiting for the bed to stop spinning so I could climb aboard the night train. He was off somewhere – probably playing that fucking Xbox with Stee – then he comes in and starts nudging me.

'You awake? You awake? You awake?'

'Well, I am now.'

Was so knackered, did the starfish – you know – (*She stretches out her arms and legs and flails about a bit.*) decked out, no energy. He's going at it like a mad thing and I don't know… Must've nodded off – only for a minute, mind – cos then I heard – 'Oh shite, Amber, it's split! Amber! Amber! Amber!'

I'm like, 'What, what, what?'

'Were you asleep?' He says, disgusted.

'Nooo, I had me eyes closed cos I was getting really into it.'

'I might as well be into necrophilia.'

At that stage I could feel my headache starting so I just said: 'Fuck off.'

But the next day I said to me ma: 'Here, what does necrophilia mean?'

The look on her face was pure horror.

'What weird shit are you getting up?'

'Ah, nothing,' says I. 'Heard it on the telly.'

It must be really bad – like when they poo on ye or something. Maybe it's his posh way of saying I'm shite in the sack. He does that sometimes, uses big words I don't understand, bet the cunt doesn't know what it means either. We hardly made a baby outta that, did we? **99**

Love and Information

Caryl Churchill

☞ **WHO**   Unspecified. We assume the speaker is a woman.

☞ **TO WHOM**   Unspecified. We assume to a lover.

☞ **WHERE**   Unspecified. We assume at the entrance to her house. You decide.

☞ **WHEN**   Present day.

☞ **WHAT HAS JUST HAPPENED**   The speech that follows is from a duologue entitled 'Manic'. It is one of over seventy short scenes that go to make up Caryl Churchill's full-length play *Love and Information*.

☞ **WHAT TO CONSIDER**

- The play is in seven sections. Within the sections there are several scenes. These scenes can be played in any order. There is no indication about what age or sex the characters are, other than the content of what is written. Here, we assume the speaker is a woman talking to her lover, for no other reason than red roses are traditionally the gift of a man to a woman. However, this need not be the case. The flowers may even be tulips or carnations, for example. Use the opportunity to create a character for yourself and make a decision about to whom exactly you are speaking.

- The scene is entitled 'Manic'. It is a clear indication of her state of mind. Make sure that you stay on top of her thoughts, however, and that the script does not run away with you. As you can see, there is only one full-stop in the speech right at the end.

- The writer cleverly captures both the joy of receiving the flowers and the resulting discombobulation about what vase to use and how they should be arranged.

- How a simple gift and, in particular, the colour red triggers her fears about life and death. Note how she struggles to convince herself that things will be all right.

- Within the play there are over one hundred other voices all trying to cope with an information overload.

☞ **WHAT SHE WANTS**

- To thank her lover.
- To reassure herself that red does not necessarily signify death and destruction.
- To reassure her lover that he/she will be quite safe.

☞ **KEYWORDS**   red   blood   anger   death

☞ **NB**   This play offers a number of other speeches from which to choose.

Unspecified

❝ My god, look at that flower, thank you so much, have you ever seen such a red, red is blood and bullfights and seeing red is anger but red is joyful, red is celebration,

[…]

in China red is lucky how lucky we are to have red flowers,

[…]

in China white is death and here black is death but ghosts are white of course so a chessboard is death against death, and blood of course could be death but it's lifeblood isn't it, if you look at the flower it's so astounding

[…]

it means so much to me that you gave me red flowers because red is so significant don't you think? it means stop and of course it means go because it's the colour of energy and red cars have the most accidents because people are excited by red or people who are already excited like to have red, I'd like to have red, I'll buy a red car this afternoon and we can go for a drive, we can go right up through the whole country don't you think, we can go to Scotland we can go to John o' Groats, did he eat a lot of porridge do you think? but we don't have to start from Land's End or Land's Beginning we should say if we start from there but we won't we'll start from here because here is always the place we start from, isn't that funny, and I need to drive along all the roads in the country because I have to see to the traffic because there are too many cars as everyone knows but our car won't be one too many you'll be quite safe, we'll make sure it's all flowing smoothly in every direction because cars do go in every direction possible and everything goes in every possible direction, so we'll find a vase for the flowers,

[…]

I think a green vase because of the primary colours and if they were blue I'd put them in an orange vase and if they were yellow I'd put them in a purple vase, yellow and purple is Easter of course so that's why crocuses, and red and green is Christmas which isn't right now of course it's the wrong time of year, I might have to sort that out when I've got a minute. **99**

Loyal Women

Gary Mitchell

☞ **WHO**   Brenda, thirty-three, Northern Irish, Protestant.

☞ **TO WHOM**   Jenny, her daughter, sixteen.

☞ **WHERE**   The living room of their house, Belfast.

☞ **WHEN**   Present day.

☞ **WHAT HAS JUST HAPPENED**   Brenda's husband and Jenny's
father, Terry, has recently been released from prison after serving
sixteen years for a crime that he did not commit. During the
course of the play we discover that it was Brenda who killed a
Catholic woman suspected of being a member of the IRA and in
order to protect Brenda (and as Brenda suggests, in order to
escape family obligations), it is Terry who falsely admits to the
crime and is charged with the woman's murder. On his release
from prison, Terry maintains that he wants to resume where he
left off – to join his wife and child and to live at last as a family,
but as soon as he is out of prison he sleeps with another woman
and Brenda is unable to forgive him. Meanwhile, Brenda has been
coerced into further dealings with the women of the Ulster
Defence Association (UDA). She has been instructed to sort out
a situation between a local Protestant girl and her Catholic
boyfriend. Jenny is impressed by the women members of the
UDA who visit Brenda and wants to join them, but Brenda
regards them as thugs and wants Jenny to have nothing to do
with them. Here Brenda attempts to explain to Jenny the truth
about what happened, the truth about her father and their
relationship and about the dangers of getting involved with the
UDA and their rough kind of justice.

☞ **WHAT TO CONSIDER**

- The history and politics of Northern Ireland. Take time to
  research these subjects, if they are not already familiar to you.
  When you have read the whole play and are clear about the
  issues raised you will have a greater understanding of Brenda's
  situation and the strength of her passion.

- The hold an organisation like the UDA can have over the local residents.

- Also living in the house are Terry's bedridden mother and Jenny's crying baby. To what extent is Brenda trapped by circumstance and also by her own sense of duty?

- In Terry's absence, Brenda has made friends with Mark, who has been doing odd jobs around the house. Although their relationship is platonic he would clearly like to become more intimate.

☞ **WHAT SHE WANTS**

- To reveal the truth about what happened. To what extent is this a relief for her? To what extent does it leave her exposed and vulnerable? Does it bring her closer to Jenny, or does it create a further rift between them? You decide.

- To tell Jenny about her relationship with Jenny's father. How easy/difficult is it for Brenda to say these things. However badly Terry has behaved, he is, after all, Jenny's father and she knows that Jenny loves him.

- To prevent her daughter from any involvement with the UDA.

- To save her daughter from making the same mistakes that she did.

- Atonement/To atone.

☞ **KEYWORDS**   owe   superhero   kill   believed   death never   head-banger   blame

Brenda

❝ Maybe I do owe him something. Jenny, your dad is a superhero. He went to prison for me because I was told by people like your new best friends who are also superheroes to go and kill a young Catholic woman who was in the IRA and coming into our area to set people up and I believed them and I did it just like I believed this superhero when he told me 'til death us do part. I suppose he left that bit out as usual. See that's the thing about him, he never tells the whole story, just the part that makes him look good. [...] I didn't know if she was in the IRA or not. I just took their word for it because I was young and I believed them. I was a teenager like you. A real head-banger but I grew up and I learned things – like how to think for myself and look after myself and how to prioritise. I used to have a list it read like this: Protestants, Ulster, the Queen, Britain and fuck everything else but I changed that list to me, my mum, my daughter and her daughter and that's the way it will stay. [...] He's trying to make you think that he did the right thing. Let me tell you what he did. He ran away from you. He didn't want me to go to prison and leave him here with you. And his mum, did I mention her? He wanted to get away from her and he wanted to get away from me and I don't really blame him we weren't a great couple obviously. But he was the great love of my life. The one and only in fact if you must know. And my other great love was my country and look how that turned out. You could say both of them have let me down. **99**

Memory

Jonathan Lichtenstein

☞ **WHO**   Eva, thirty, a Jew.

☞ **TO WHOM**   Felix, a Nazi.

☞ **WHERE**   An allotment, Berlin, Germany.

☞ **WHEN**   1942, night-time, winter.

☞ **WHAT HAS JUST HAPPENED**   The play starts with a group of actors rehearsing a play. There are two strands to the play: the story of Eva, a German Jew; and the story of Isaac and Bashar, a young Israeli and an elderly Palestinian. Eva's story takes us from 1933 to 1990, after the fall of the Berlin Wall. The narrative moves backwards and forwards in time and sometimes stops as the actors within the play take breaks. At this point in the story, Eva is married to Aron, and they have three boys, their own son and two who are the sons of Eva's cousin. Before the war, Felix was their friend. With the rise of Fascism and subsequent outbreak of war, Felix has joined the Nazi Party and is now Eva and Aron's enemy. In this scene, Felix has come to the allotment where Aron and Eva are in hiding following a tip-off from one of their neighbours. He has come to arrest them. He demands to know why there are only two children with them. Aron tells him that their own son is now in England and that they only had enough money to send one child on the Kindertransport. Felix asks, 'So you chose your own child?... Tell me what happened.' Eva's speech here is her response to him.

☞ **WHAT TO CONSIDER**

- The historical background. Take time to familiarise yourself with the plight of the German Jews and, in particular, the Kindertransport that enabled Jewish children to flee Germany.

- Before the war, Felix was in love with Eva and was hurt and angry when she chose to marry Aron.

- Aron and Felix at one time shared a successful shoe business.

- After this speech Eva offers to let Felix sleep with her if he will let them all go. Read the play to find out whether he keeps his word.

☞ WHAT SHE WANTS

- To describe as best she can her feeling of loss. Note how visceral her memory is.
- To appeal to Felix's sense of humanity.
- For Felix to spare them.

☞ KEYWORDS   body   cream   hair   scalp   perfume   skin   nostrils   hand

Eva

❝ The train went from here to the Hook of Holland and then to Harwich. I persuaded myself he was going on holiday and that he would be back soon. It's what I told him. Before he left I bathed him. He was five and so his body was like cream. I washed his hair, he complained, but it was for me, not for him and I scratched his scalp and cascaded warm water over him, I knew it was the last time. I held him tight and the hot perfume of his skin entered my nostrils. I dressed him and we picked up his bags and I carried one and he the other. We caught a tram and I took him to the barrier at the Grunewaldstrasse where all the other children were. There his hand slipped mine. It surprised me, the speed. I tried to keep my eyes on him but he was whisked away. The officials took him. I waved the train goodbye. It was laden with children. Some of them smiled and waved. After it left, there were hundreds of parents left on the platform. We were so quiet. We were Jews and we didn't want any attention on ourselves. I walked home. It took me hours. When I returned to the flat, the water was still in the bath. It had gone cold but I couldn't let it out. I lay on his bed and I covered myself with his clothes.

Beat.

What can we give you to let us go? […]

EVA *takes off her coat and unbuttons her dress.*

[…] It's what you want. […] Take me, Felix. […] Take me.
Any way you like. […] Take me. Then let me go. Take me and
let us all go. In the shed. Now. Let yourself. Look at you. I
know you want to and now you can. You can have me. Finally.
I'm all yours. To the victor the spoils. **99**

Mogadishu

Vivienne Franzmann

☞ **WHO**   Becky, fourteen, white.

☞ **TO WHOM**   Peter, her stepfather, forties, black.

☞ **WHERE**   Their kitchen.

☞ **WHEN**   Present day.

☞ **WHAT HAS JUST HAPPENED**   Becky goes to the same school where her mother Amanda is a teacher. Amanda has recently been suspended from teaching there. She was trying to break up a fight between a black boy called Jason and a Turkish boy called Firat. During the fracas, Amanda was knocked to the ground by Jason. She was reluctant to make an official complaint, fearing it would result in Jason's permanent exclusion from the school. In the meantime, however, Jason has accused Amanda of racially abusing him and of pushing him. While the school investigates the truth of Jason's allegations it has been decided that Amanda should stay at home. Jason's father, Ben, is adamant that his son is telling the truth, and it is not long before the police are involved and the incident is subject to a criminal investigation. All this has placed a huge strain on Amanda, her husband Peter and Becky. Here, Becky, who is not sleeping well and is late for school, has been joined for breakfast in the kitchen by Peter, her stepfather. Becky asks Peter whether he remembers when he first met her and what she was like. He tells her that she was sad and that for six whole months she did not speak. She is surprised at this. She does not remember. There is a silence between them and then Becky asks 'Did you ever see the old pier in Brighton?' The speech that follows is made up of the conversation they then have.

☞ **WHAT TO CONSIDER**

- Becky's father committed suicide. The tie to which she refers is the one that he used to hang himself. It was her Christmas present to him.

- On some level she blames herself for her father's death.

- Becky self-harms. She cuts herself. Her arms and legs are a criss-cross of scars.

- Peter describes her as brave, funny and clever. Later on in the play she courageously confronts Jason in order to try to persuade him to tell the truth.

☞ WHAT SHE WANTS

- To explain her six-month silence.

- To explain her depression.

- To relive a memory that has taken on an even greater significance owing to the strangeness of the photograph. To what extent is her need to do this related to her feelings of guilt and her compulsion to self-harm?

- To distance herself from Peter (he is not her real father) but at the same time to seek comfort and reassurance from him that she is not a bad person.

☞ KEYWORDS   obsessed   deteriorating   weirdo   cheesy
headless

Becky

❝ Did you ever see the old pier in Brighton? […] My dad was obsessed by it. […] He was always going on about how it was deteriorating. He used to take a photo of it every week so he had a record of it falling down. What a weirdo. […] I've got this photo of me and him standing in front of it. This really old woman took it. Dad asked her to and she was shaking because she was nervous in case she took it wrong. He bought her a cup of tea after and he kept making her laugh calling her 'lady in red' and 'scarlet woman' because she had this red coat on. He could be really cheesy sometimes. I mean really fucking cheesy.

Pause.

And then we walked her back to her house and when we got there, she bent right down and took my hand and said, 'You're very lucky to have such a wonderful daddy.'

Pause.

Talk about cheesy. That is cheese on toast. That whole story is mature cheddar on a piece of poor-little-me toast. [...] If I close my eyes, I can see that woman so clearly. I can remember everything about her. Everything.

Pause.

But when I think of Dad, I can't see him. It's like he's getting further and further away from me and the more I try, the more I try to imagine, the more I look at photos of him to try and remember, the stranger he looks. [...] When we got the pictures back, she'd cut his head off. In the photo I'm holding hands with a headless man. **99**

Mother Teresa is Dead

Helen Edmundson

☞ **WHO**   Jane, late twenties – 'she has a strong regional accent (from somewhere that places her well away from London)'.

☞ **TO WHOM**   Mark, her husband, Frances, a middle-aged English woman with whom she is staying in Chennai, Srinivas, an Indian man who runs the children's shelter where she has been working.

☞ **WHERE**   The studio of Frances's house in a village near Chennai, India, where Mark and Jane have been sleeping on the sofa bed.

☞ **WHEN**   Present day.

☞ **WHAT HAS JUST HAPPENED**   Before the play starts, Jane, having left her husband and five-year-old son without warning, has been travelling around India compelled by an impulsive desire to help those in need. When she arrives at Chennai Central Station, she meets Srinivas, an Oxford-educated Indian man, and goes to work in his shelter for street children. She is also taken in by Frances, an artist, who offers her somewhere to stay. During this time she has been clinging on to a white plastic carrier bag the contents of which are a mystery to us. She says there is a baby in the bag, but Frances knows that cannot be true. At the start of the play, Jane's husband Mark arrives at Frances's house. Jane has asked Frances to contact him, and he has travelled from London in order to take her back home. She has been absent for seven weeks, and Mark wants to know why she left. She explains how she needed to 'get back to something simple… to get down on my knees and help someone who couldn't help themselves'. She misses her son, but is unsure about whether to go back with Mark. One night while they are asleep on the sofa bed, Jane has a nightmare. Her crying wakes up the household. She is talking about having killed a baby. Srinivas asks her what she means. The speech that follows is Jane's response.

☞ WHAT TO CONSIDER

- At the end of Jane's speech, Srinivas picks up the plastic bag and takes it to Jane. Inside there is a brown envelope containing a passport, a wedding ring and some money. Jane is forced to remember how the woman would not take them. 'She thought I was trying to buy her baby. She wouldn't let him go. Not for my whole world.' In this way we realise that the tale of the baby is a kind of delusion/fiction and that Jane's ability to distinguish truth from fiction/illusion has been blurred. It is important however that you play the speech for real.

- Make a decision about how and why she convinced herself that she had killed the baby.

- Jane is highly sensitive. Decide to what extent her creative and imaginative personality is in some way linked to her tendency toward depression.

- The courage of a woman who, however misguided, is prepared to put thought into action.

- Read the play to find out whether she decides to stay in India or to go back to London.

☞ WHAT SHE WANTS

- To make confession.

- Forgiveness or (given her state of mind) punishment. You decide.

☞ KEYWORDS   thin   tiny   safe   care   nothing   need   dry   hard   flat   dead

Jane

❝ The woman in the shanty town, with the thin baby. I gave her my passport and my keys and my rings and she gave me her baby. And it tucked itself into my neck, like a tiny bat. And I started to walk. I walked and walked to find a safe place for the baby, because I have to take care of this baby. It's dark, it's night and now there are people behind me. There are people. They're following me through the streets. And I walk faster and I almost drop the baby and I put it into my bag to keep it safe. And I run. And I reach a shore. It is the sea. And now I can see them. They're coming from the darkness. They're boys. They're only boys. Each one's older than the one before. They're begging from me – 'Medam Medam, Medam Medam'. They're running around me. They're excited. Their eyes are shining. They're laughing and doing somersaults. And they start to touch me, tugging at my sleeves, just touching, slightly, 'Medam Medam'. 'I can't,' I say, 'I've got nothing'. 'Medam Medam,' they tap their mouths. They point down into their throats, their throats are like caves. They pull at me now, 'Medam Medam'. I lift the bag above my head to keep the baby safe. I'm panicking – 'I've got nothing', they love it, my fear, it's thrilling them. The youngest one's on the ground, he has his hands around my legs, 'Medam Medam'. I drag him, with every step I drag him along the sand. He's laughing, the older boys are laughing, pulling at my skin and hair. I try to get his fingers off my ankles but they're so strong, they're strong with need. 'Get off me. Get off me'. I free my leg, my leg's free and I kick, I kick his head, hard. I kick. His fingers come off me. He falls back. There's nothing. There's shock. Then he smiles, and sits up and rubs his head, like he's in a cartoon and the boys laugh and laugh and I run. I run fast, with the bag against my chest. And when I stop it's almost light and I'm in a square. And I sit on the ground, the stone ground, and I open up the bag and I put my hand inside to take out the baby, the baby... but it is dead. It's dry and hard and flat. It's dead. **"**

My Name is Rachel Corrie

Taken from the writings of Rachel Corrie
Edited by Alan Rickman and Katherine Viner

☞ **WHO**   Rachel Corrie, twenty-three, American. (In the speech below, she is still a teenager.)

☞ **TO WHOM**   The audience (see note on 'Direct audience address' in the introduction).

☞ **WHERE**   Rachel's bedroom. Olympia, Washington, USA.

☞ **WHEN**   Some time before January 2003.

☞ **WHAT HAS JUST HAPPENED**   The speech that follows comes close to the start of a play about the true-life story of Rachel Corrie. In January 2003, aged twenty-three, Rachel left home to join the International Solidarity Movement in Gaza. She was killed on 16th March 2003, when an Israeli bulldozer ran her down as she was attempting to protect a Palestinian home. The play is made up from extracts of her journals and emails. At this point in the story, Rachel is still at school.

☞ **WHAT TO CONSIDER**

- The extraordinary braveness of a young woman who is prepared to fight and die for what she believes in.

- From an early age, Rachel was politicised. She held strong and passionate views about human rights.

- Her trip to Russia is a seminal experience. It is after this that she develops her 'wanderlust'.

- The Israeli/Palestinian conflict. Take time to familiarise yourself with the arguments. It is hugely complex and, as it was for Rachel, not an easy thing to understand.

- The play takes the form of one long monologue.

☞ **WHAT SHE WANTS**

- To introduce herself. Note how she identifies herself as the 'outsider'.

- To describe her need for experiences beyond the everyday.

- To express her growing disquiet with things American.

- To explain her restlessness.

☞ **KEYWORDS**   naked   fire   belly   dirty   pretty   flawed
broken   gorgeous   awake   sob   home

☞ **NB**   This play offers a number of other speeches from
which to choose.

Rachel

❝ Okay. I'm Rachel. Sometimes I wear ripped blue jeans.
Sometimes I wear polyester. Sometimes I take off all my
clothes and swim naked at the beach. I don't believe in fate
but my astrological sign is Aries, the ram, and my sign on the
Chinese zodiac is the sheep, and the name Rachel means
sheep but I've got a fire in my belly. It used to be such a big
loud blazing fire that I couldn't hear anybody else over it. So I
talked a lot and I didn't listen too much. Then I went to
middle school where you gotta be *cool* and you gotta be *strong*
and *tough*, and I tried real hard to be cool. But luckily, luckily
I happened to get a free trip to Russia and I saw another
country for the first time.

In the streets and the alleys it was an obstacle course of
garbage and mud and graffiti. There was coal dust on the
snow, everything was dirty. And they always said to us, 'How
do you like our dirty city?' Oh, but it was so pretty with the
little lights in the windows and the red dusk-light on the
buildings. It was flawed, dirty, broken and gorgeous.

I looked backwards across the Pacific Ocean and from that
distance some things back here in Olympia, Washington, USA
seemed a little weird and disconcerting. But I was awake in
Russia. I was awake for the first time with bug-eyes and a grin.

On the flight home from Anchorage to Seattle everything was
dark. Then the sun began to rise, the water was shining, and

I realised we were flying over Puget Sound. Soon we could see islands in that water, evergreen trees on those islands.

And I began to sob. I sobbed in all that radiance, in the midst of the most glorious sunrise I'd ever seen, because it wasn't enough. It wasn't enough to make me glad to be home. **")**

My Name is Tania Head*

Alexandra Wood

☞ **WHO**   Tania Head, 9/11 survivor, Spanish.

☞ **TO WHOM**   The audience, whom she addresses as members of the World Trade Center Survivors' Network.

☞ **WHERE**   A meeting room of some kind.

☞ **WHEN**   2003.

☞ **WHAT HAS JUST HAPPENED**   The speech forms the start of a longer monologue based on the experiences of 9/11 'survivor', 'Tania Head'.

☞ **WHAT TO CONSIDER**

- In reality, Tania Head was a fake. Her real name was and is Alicia Esteve Head. She was in Barcelona at the time of the attack but came to prominence in 2003 when she claimed to be one of only nineteen people to survive the explosion above where the second airplane entered the South Tower. She subsequently became President of the World Trade Center Survivors' Network. She was exposed in 2007 when her true identity was revealed.

- There are many theories as to why she decided to make up such a thing. Research her.

- In the speech she talks of her right arm being on fire. Alicia had a pre-existing injury to her right arm which she was able to use to create the lie.

- Decide to what extent you wish to play Alicia playing 'Tania'.

☞ **WHAT SHE WANTS**

- To find a sense of belonging.
- To be loved (the story of Dave is complete fiction).
- To be admired and noticed.

* Published in the volume *Decade*

- To help (despite her web of lies, she was an effective campaigner for those who had survived).

☞ **KEYWORDS** glad here survive family relief help forgotten

Tania

❝ My name is Tania Head.

I come from Spain, originally, but I've lived in New York for five years now, and I consider it my home. I do.

I'm glad to be here.

I'm glad to be here. That was something I learnt to say. When I did my course in Business English. I'm glad to be here. Insert at the start of presentation.

But when I say it today I mean it.

I am, truly, glad to be here, because I was on the seventy-eighth floor of the South Tower that day, and I could, very easily, have not been here now. I was one of only nineteen people above where the plane hit to survive.

I am glad to be here.

Although I'm only meeting you for the first time, you already feel like a kind of family. When I found your site and read what you've written about your experiences that day it was such a relief.

Shall I tell my story, is that something you – […]

I should start with Dave. He was my fiancé and my best friend. We met when we both went for the same cab. I was in a rush, so was he, who isn't, so we shared it. And we shared almost everything else from then on. It was the first week that I was here. When I wrote and told my friends in Spain, I've met an American man, in a yellow cab, they thought I was joking. And I said, no, it happens! Even to someone like me. Dave was all-American, the athletic type, he played basketball in college, he was gorgeous. And he made me feel like the most beautiful woman on earth. So you can see how special he was.

He was killed in the North Tower, where he worked.

I was in the South Tower, as I said, on the seventy-eighth floor. When I looked around, just after it hit, it was like a horror movie. I was choking on the smell of burnt skin and people's insides. And I realised my right arm was on fire. It's funny, what came to me is what I learnt at school. I threw myself to the floor, and rolled to put it out.

She raises the right arm of her cardigan to reveal a scar.

The doctors have been wonderful.

In amongst all the chaos, all the screaming and the panic, I kept thinking about my white wedding dress, and swearing my love for Dave, we were supposed to get married that October, and I believe it was him, on his way to Heaven, who led me out of there. I just kept thinking of our wedding day, and it kept me alive.

In Spain we have a saying, *a Dios rogando y con el mazo dando*. You have something similar, God helps those who help themselves. We should help each other. At the moment we have to stand outside the site with the tourists and the souvenir sellers. It's disgraceful. I would like to do what I can to secure access to Ground Zero, for those of us who feel it would help in the grieving process.

I worked for Merrill Lynch, that's what I was doing in the North Tower. I want to use whatever skills I have for, for good, I suppose.

We shouldn't be forgotten. I know I sound like a politician, and God knows we've had enough of them, but, I think it's very important.

We shouldn't be forgotten. **99**

No Romance

Nancy Harris

☞ **WHO**   Laura, thirty-six, from Dublin.

☞ **TO WHOM**   Gail, thirty-six, a photographer.

☞ **WHERE**   Gail's studio.

☞ **WHEN**   Present day. Morning.

☞ **WHAT HAS JUST HAPPENED**   Laura has breast cancer. She is
soon to start her treatment and thinks it will be best to end her
one-year relationship with her boyfriend Simon. Before she does so,
and with his fortieth birthday approaching, she wants to give him a
present to remember her by. An album of sexy photographs of
herself. She has contacted Gail, a girl with whom she was at school
and who is now a professional photographer known for her work
of Dublin's red-light district. As the play starts, Laura is dressed as
King Arthur's wife 'Guinevere'. She has brought to the shoot a bag
full of dressing-up clothes. She wants Gail to photograph her in
various guises. She has a corset that Simon bought for her which
she wants to team with a top hat and hot pants for a 'Moulin Rouge'
effect. During the course of the session, Laura breaks down and tells
Gail about the cancer. Gail is not convinced that any of these looks
or poses is the best approach and thinks that Laura would be better
off having some nude shots taken. Laura does not want this; she has
not told Simon about the cancer, and she believes a present of a
photograph of her in the nude would be like asking Simon to say
goodbye to her body. She explains to Gail, 'I want to be sexy. I want
to be strong. I want to be the woman he bought this corset for.' She
finally reveals to Gail that she has no intention of telling Simon
about the cancer. She will give him the album, celebrate his birthday
and then leave him.

☞ **WHAT TO CONSIDER**

- Laura believes she is dying. Her mother died of cancer. She
  knows that at the age of thirty-six the disease can be
  aggressive. However, Laura will quickly resort to humour to
  cover her pain, refusing to see herself as a victim.

- Gail is gay. Her ten-year relationship with her partner has ended badly. Decide to what extent that, at thirty-six, both women are having to confront the fact that life has either turned out or not turned out as they had hoped, feared or expected.

- Laura and Gail were not close at school. During the course of the play, as their loneliness is revealed, they become strangely bonded.

- Queen Medb of Connaught is a warrior queen from the 'epic pre-Christian Irish story, *The Táin Bó Cúailnge*.

☞ **WHAT SHE WANTS**

- To preserve the moment before she must undergo surgery. Decide to what extent the album is as much for her as it is for Simon. A memory of herself for herself.

- To capture an image of herself before she starts treatment.

- To avoid the mess and pain of a failed relationship.

- To maintain her dignity.

☞ **KEYWORDS**   out of the blue   fairytale   happily-ever-after
rescue   cleanly   broken

Laura

❝ I don't know if I will tell him. Simon. Ever. […] I mean… if I give Simon a picture of me – naked for his birthday and then I go and tell him I have cancer, isn't that like – isn't that like I'm asking him to say goodbye to my body? […] I don't want to say goodbye to my body. […] So why would I want him to say goodbye to my body. I want to be sexy. I want to be strong. I want to be the woman he bought this corset for – I don't want to be my mother lying in a box. And if I don't tell him, he won't know – […] Not if I leave him. […] The thing you need to understand is – I didn't think I'd meet a man like Simon. I didn't think I'd meet anyone, to be honest. I hit thirty-five. And I thought – that's it, I'm done. I'm not even looking any more because it's never going to happen. I'm just one of those people. I'm just one of those people who is meant to be on their own and that's fine. I like my job, I have my friends – who needs a fella? And then – out of the blue, Simon. And he's great. And we fall in love and he wants to marry me and spend the rest of his life with me and it's like – it's like every fucking fairytale you've ever bloody read. It's like happily-ever-after multiplied by ten – because Simon's a good man. He really is. If I tell him, he'll be fantastic. He'll drive me to radiotherapy, he'll help me change bandages, he'll bring me breakfast in bed – but he'll be doing it knowing I've a lump in my breast. He'll be doing it knowing I've cancer. […] And even though I love all these – stories about Guinevere and Medb and what have you – I've never wanted anyone to rescue me. Not like that. Not from cancer. So I figure if I do this photo album and I give him a great birthday – a birthday he can never forget and then I end it – cleanly – before they take me into hospital next week… Things can stay just the way they are. Now. Before it all gets – […] broken.

Beat.

And then I'll always get to be the woman he bought this corset for. And I'd like that. I'd like to – know that. **"**

Pandas

Rona Munro

☞ **WHO**   Lin Han, nineteen, Chinese.

☞ **TO WHOM**   Madeleine, a forty-something woman, who has just shot her ex-partner, and James, a police officer – although, because she is speaking Chinese, he cannot understand her.

☞ **WHERE**   The interview room of a police station in Edinburgh, Scotland.

☞ **WHEN**   Present day.

☞ **WHAT HAS JUST HAPPENED**   Lin Han, who works for a rug company in China, has travelled to Edinburgh to establish further links with a distribution company which is looking to import Chinese goods. Over an eighteen-month period and before she arrives, she has exchanged emails and jpegs with Jie Hui, a young Chinese man who works for the British distribution firm. During that time she has fallen in love with him, and when she arrives in the UK she hopes that he will feel the same. Before the play starts, they have been up all night talking, and when we, the audience, first meet them, she is still questioning him about his feelings towards her. He tells her he cannot feel the same way, that it is too soon and that he would like to slow down a bit. He then has to go to meet Alan, his business partner, and suggests to Lin Han that she meet with him and Alan an hour later. Alan has forgotten to bring the keys to his office, and, while he and Jie Hui are trying to gain entry, Alan is shot in the bottom by Alan's ex-girlfriend Madeleine. But when Lin Han shows up at the allotted time and Alan is lying injured, she is convinced it is Jie Hui who has tried to kill him. While Madeleine is being questioned about the attack by James, a police officer, Lin Han rushes into the police station claiming that Jie Hui is guilty of the murder. She is speaking in Mandarin and no one can understand her. Madeleine, who is an entomologist and has spent much time in China studying the lice that are found in the fur of giant pandas, happens to speak Mandarin. As there is no interpreter available at such short notice, and in need of more information about the attack, James asks Madeleine if she will translate.

☞ **WHAT TO CONSIDER**

- Although the speech is in English, Lin Han is actually speaking in Mandarin Chinese. You don't therefore need to speak with a heavy Chinese accent or in broken English. You may even wish to speak with a standard English accent or your own regional dialect.

- The play follows the stories of six characters whose lives are strangely interwoven. Read the play to understand all of the connections.

☞ **WHAT SHE WANTS**

- To report Jie Hui. However much she loves him, she feels compelled to tell the truth.

- To share her story. People in love often need to talk about it.

- Comfort and reassurance, despite the fact that she knows she has been foolish. Decide to what extent Madeleine's presence, being a woman, allows her to be open about her feelings.

☞ **KEYWORDS**   upset   happy   smile   joke   marry   sad   angry   crying   love   horrible   crazy   real

Lin Han

❝ I am Wang Lin Han. I am nineteen years old. I am here as a representative of the Panda Joy rug company. This is my passport. This is my visa.

I'm sorry. My English is very good but I'm upset. […] I'm very upset and I can't think of the words. […] I am our company's international representative. Because of my language skills. […] I have been in communication with the representative of a distribution company. He finds contacts and investors to distribute the products of small-scale Chinese manufacturing companies into Europe. […] Sometimes I wrote to this man in our language and sometimes we wrote in

English, to practise. We had a very... happy correspondence, we made each other smile... at least... he put smileys in his messages too. So after a few months my father made a joke. He said this man would be the perfect husband for me because it would be so good for the family business. You see my father and my mother would like me to marry very soon but they know I think I shouldn't get married before I'm thirty. So they say things like that, as if they're joking, but I know they mean it too. [...] So I stopped the messages with the smileys in them. It was all business. And then he sent me another message with sad faces, and he asked if I was angry with him... [...] I thought, I've studied English for so long because I wanted to travel. And here I was just working in the same little factory I grew up in, in the same little town. I thought, this man could help me travel. It *would* be great for business so my mum and dad would be happy, I could escape without anyone crying about it.

And I've been in love and it was really horrible. It's really horrible to want someone and be in their power like that. [...] So... I thought I should think about a relationship with this man. It would be a practical choice. It would get me what I want. I asked him to send me a picture. [...] It was a beautiful picture. I loved his picture. [...] And it wasn't a studio picture! It wasn't lit and airbrushed and all shined up in Photoshop. It was just a casual picture. He was on the beach. He was smiling at me with such a look... [...] I fell in love with his picture. I have to be honest now. I hoped he would love me first but that's what happened. I fell in love with a picture and a set of letters. Like a crazy girl who doesn't know what's real. [...] He was right. He was right, I know nothing about him. And now I love him. Do you know the story about the baby ducks? [...] The first thing a baby duck sees moving when it breaks through its shell it will love as its mother. You can make them love cats that want to eat them or chase after bicycle wheels and die in the road. I was just breaking out into the world. I'm a baby duck and I'm following a killer. [...] I saw him with the body of this man. He said it had nothing to do with him, he was talking and talking and I looked in his eyes and I saw a lie.

Now I've realised I'm a stupid little duckling with shell in my baby feathers. I've stepped out into the world and it'll squash me. I thought I knew how to do anything but I'm just a stupid little girl. […] And I really do love him. Even though he probably is a killer and a liar. **99**

Perve

Stacey Gregg

☞ **WHO**   Layla, eighteen, Southern Irish.

☞ **TO WHOM**   A police officer.

☞ **WHERE**   A police station.

☞ **WHEN**   Present day.

☞ **WHAT HAS JUST HAPPENED**   This is the only time that Layla appears in the play. She has decided to go to the police following rumours that her ex-boyfriend Nick's best friend, Gethin, is a pervert. As she explains in the speech that follows, she believes Nick showed Gethin a naked photograph he took of her and that Gethin shared it. Layla does not refer to Gethin by name, but as 'him' or 'he'.

☞ **WHAT TO CONSIDER**

- We don't know much about Layla except that:

  She has a little sister who is called 'Electrolux' at school, because, like Layla, she is considered frigid.

  Her father is described as a 'Bible basher'.

  She dated Nick.

  She took time off school when her naked picture was posted online.

- Use this opportunity to create a fully rounded character for yourself.

- Although it is acutely embarrassing, decide to what extent she might be enjoying the attention that this opportunity has afforded her. Is it an easy story for her to recount or is it painful?

☞ **WHAT SHE WANTS**

- Justice.

- Revenge.

- To protect others from what she herself went through.

☞ **KEYWORDS**   embarrassed   stupid   sweet   chivalrou
messing   alien   beautiful   muppet   muses   mortifying
disappear   bent

Layla

❝ sorry, yeah.

Uhh. It's something – it's something I never. I never did
nothing about it then – at the time – cos I – you know I was
embarrassed. Stupid. Stupid to have… But then I didn't
think. I didn't know. He was – I went out with him for like,
seven months, which is like for ever when you're like sixteen.
And he was older so it was really, like, cool. He had a Corsa.
He was really nice. I don't really – I don't think he would've
meant to… he was – I donno – must've been twenty-one?
Twenty. Four years older. Well, three and a half. But he was so
sweet, he never made me feel little, you know? You know what,
he didn't even sleep with me. Swear to God. Even though we
went out for so long, isn't that cool? Amazing? In this day and
age. I mean, we lied, we said we'd done it cos otherwise his
friends would've been assholes. Mine too. But we never did.
Well, we did eventually, like after we broke up, like. Anyway.
Kind of. Chivalrous or something. But the phones with
cameras, everyone has them now. They've got like super-
cameras like underwater optical-zoom fifty-megapixel shit and
stuff – sorry – I've a really nice Nokia – but those were only
out really, the good ones, when we were going out. Nick had
one. We were messing about, just. You know. And it was really
hot. Really hot I think, he had his T-shirt off first. We were,
you know. Messing about. And I took my top off, it was a top
from H&M, nice maroon vest so it was. I took it off you know
and my bra – I mean it is, it was half my fault – and he took
this stupid fucking picture – and I was like 'delete it! Gross! I
look like an ALIEN or something!' But he was like 'no, it's
beautiful.' He said – I know I'm a muppet – but at the time it
was so like – he said it would be like in olden times when they
carried little portraits and sexy pictures of their muses or

something – seriously don't know where he came up with that stuff – so he didn't delete it. Like, I don't know, I seriously don't know how it came to be... I mean, all I know is that the only other person who had such a snazzy phone, or who would've had like, access to Nick's or who – and I can't believe he would – but if Nick *did* show him – he swears to God he didn't – but I mean, I was out of school for like two months. I had to repeat after the summer. And starting a new school in September was like, the most mortifying, humiliating thing I've ever had to do. Some of the teachers knew, but they didn't really know how to deal with it I think. It wasn't in the papers or anything the way it is now – they had other problems you know? And I didn't want any action taken – I just wanted to like, disappear. It felt like – like –

I just wanted it to disappear.

Or for me to disappear.

I don't know.

God. I – it felt so... *uhhgh*.

I tried to disappear – if you know what I mean...[...]

... everything felt so shit. But. He did that. I know it was him. He was always so pervy – he always carried this fucking video camera around with him. I don't know. So when someone said – the other day someone said about how they'd heard he was – you know, like – bent or something. I thought. I don't want anyone else to go through that. I told my mum. She said I should come here. Not for me. Not so much. But in case there're others. In case it wasn't a one-off, you know? I don't want to waste anyone's time. I just thought. You know? I should. You know? Say. **99**

Pieces

Hywel John

☞ **WHO**   Bea, a pre-adolescent child.

☞ **TO WHOM**   Sophie, her godmother.

☞ **WHERE**   The sitting room of a family house, in a remote part of the countryside.

☞ **WHEN**   Present day.

☞ **WHAT HAS JUST HAPPENED**   Bea and her twin brother Jack have lost their parents in a car accident. The only person who is able to look after them is Sophie, their godmother. Sophie has not seen them in years, and they can barely remember her. Bea can just about recall Sophie from a birthday party the twins had when they were very little. She has an abiding memory of her mother shouting at her father afterwards. The play starts straight after the funeral. Sophie has come to stay in their large house on the edge of the forest. The three of them are in shock and are struggling to come to terms with what has just happened. It is shortly before dawn after their second night together and Bea has woken up early. She is wearing her mother's floral dress and has come downstairs to the sitting room where Sophie is asleep on the couch. She practises her ballet, and Sophie wakes up. She explains to Sophie that she is not very good at ballet and that Jack thinks she is a 'clodhopper'. She asks Sophie if she will dance with her.

☞ WHAT TO CONSIDER

- Bea is grieving the sudden loss of her parents.
- She is one of a twin.
- Her relationship with her brother is strange and intense.
- Although they are children, both Bea and Jack are highly articulate and very direct. They like to dress as adults and mimic their parents' relationship. (Later in the play Sophie is shocked to see the twins kissing.)

- Like many twins there is something self-sufficient about Bea and Jack that others find unnerving. Decide to what extent growing up in such a remote place has influenced them.

- The constant power struggle between Sophie and the twins.

- Read the play to find out why Sophie has been absent from the family for so long and to discover what happens when the twins prepare a 'surprise' birthday party for themselves.

☞ **WHAT SHE WANTS**

- To imagine her mother is still alive.

- To hang on to what is familiar and normal by recreating the family routine.

- To find a way forward.

☞ **KEYWORDS**   wake/woke   early   kiss   pieces   puzzle
quiz   game

Bea

❝ Will you do dancing with me, Sophie? […] Oh, come on. […] I don't care. I'm a clodhopper, so you'll only be as bad as me. […] Come on, come on, come on. […] Sometimes I wake up this early and come down and I see Mum standing right here, looking out at the sun rising on the garden. She wears this dress sometimes when I've seen her. I'm in my jim–jams though.

She stands here all quiet just looking out of the window and I know she's just like me because she obviously woke up straight away very early too just like me. I stand still and look at her sometimes. Mostly I say hello and she gives me a kiss and walks into the kitchen and puts the kettle on. Then I do my dancing practice.

Dad and Jack are fast asleep and they never saw it. Not once. But Mum comes back in with her tea and watches me here. In this spot, right here, watching me be a right old clodhopper. Then once she finishes her tea she comes over and helps me a bit. And we dance together a bit. Then she gives me a kiss and goes to wake up Dad.

So, come on. Come on, Sophie. Then I'll go and wake up Jack. […] Just hold my hands as I practise pirouetting on my tiptoes. […]

We have to fill the gaps. […] Like a jigsaw. […] Jack and me were talking about it. […] Is that what the phrase 'picking up the pieces' means? […]

We read it in some book. It said something like: 'When something as terrible as this happens, only the children are left to pick up the pieces.' Something like that. And I thought, what pieces do I have to pick up? And I've been looking around and I think it's like a jigsaw puzzle, where you have to pick up all the pieces to complete the picture all over again. And we just got to figure out what those pieces are. It's like a quiz. Like a game of hide-and-seek or something. I'm going to have a morning bath now. […] Put the kettle on. Mum puts the kettle on. 🙶

Precious Little Talent

Ella Hickson

☞ **WHO**   Joey, twenty-three, middle class, English.

☞ **TO WHOM**   The audience (see note on 'Direct audience address' in the introduction).

☞ **WHERE**   New York.

☞ **WHEN**   February, 2009.

☞ **WHAT HAS JUST HAPPENED**   Joey has flown to New York to visit her father George, whom she has not seen in two years. Up on the rooftop above his apartment she meets Sam, a nineteen-year-old American boy. It is Christmas Eve and they spend a madcap evening chasing up and down Manhattan together. The following morning, Sam and Joey are surprised to see each other in George's apartment. Sam had no idea that Joey was George's daughter, and Joey, thinking that Sam is just a friendly neighbour, has no idea that Sam is George's carer or that George is suffering from Lewy body dementia. Both men try to keep her unaware of George's condition, but it becomes obvious on Christmas Day when, during a game of Trivial Pursuit, George, a former academic, cannot remember the answer to a simple question. Later when they are alone, Joey quizzes Sam about George's life expectancy. He tells her that it is between three to five years. Joey is terrified that her father will forget her. In the meantime, Sam has fallen in love with Joey, but Joey is much more reserved. The play then fast-forwards to February, which is when she tells us – in the speech that follows – about how their relationship has developed.

☞ **WHAT TO CONSIDER**

- Joey has left university with a first-class degree. She was sacked from a bar job. Like many of her generation, she cannot find suitable work.

- She cannot relate to her mother, who has remarried a Muslim man and with whom she has had a daughter who speaks a different language.

- Joey is terrified of insignificance and says she is scared she will 'disappear'.

- Is Joey's angst synonymous with that of being twenty-something or has it more to do with the fact that her father is dying?

- Joey's cynicism is typically English, while Sam's brand of optimism is typically American.

- Much of the play's discussion and humour resides in the differences between English and American sensibilities.

- Barack Obama is 'that new President of theirs'.

☞ WHAT SHE WANTS

- To believe in something bigger than herself.

- For something to matter to her.

- To live a life that is meaningful.

- To make a difference and to be remembered.

☞ KEYWORDS   movement   soul   faith   believe   forgotten

Joey

❝ It's a movement, isn't it? That's what they call it. When people feel the same thing in their soul at the same time – they call it a movement. I've always been jealous that I never got to ban the bomb, or burn my bras, jealous of people that lived through the war because, well, they had a common enemy and that'd make you want to fight and it'd make it clear what you were fighting for and it might even allow for a hero or two.

I said this to Sam, who, it transpired, one got used to over time – sure there were differences; sex, for example. I liked the British kind, angsty, passionate but essentially joyless and for him, well it was sort of like going to the Oscars, lots of tears and thank-yous and I felt he struggled with an overwhelming urge to clap at the end.

We sat with Dad, and played board games and talked and – Sam would take over when Dad forgot things, or when I found dirty plates in the cupboard or his shaving stuff in the cutlery drawer, or once when he struggled for my name – Sam stepped in at times when I just couldn't really stop myself from finding it all horribly sad. (*Controls tears.*)

In January Sam took me away for the weekend – and when we got to Washington, strangers were high-fiving each other and smiling and everyone seemed so – excited. It was that same feeling I'd had, on that rooftop on Christmas Day, right in the pit of my stomach, looking at all those tiny lights holding tiny lives and knowing that they were part of something – but that something was bigger than them – and it was good. And when it came to it, with the sun peeking itself out behind the Washington Monument, and looking down The Mall and seeing two million people waiting, exercising the muscle of – faith – well, I thought that it didn't really matter what you believed in – just as long as you knew how to believe.

And just as he appeared and all the flags started waving and young kids started whooping and older men and women shed some quieter tears, Sam turned to me and he wrapped me right up in his scarf and he said –

'Now, you've got to believe in this – right?'

And I looked at him, and he had this stupid smile on his face, grinning ear to fucking ear, and suddenly I realised what kind of balls it takes just to think that the world isn't such a bad place.

But of course, Sam, Dad, even that new President of theirs, they weren't really mine to believe in, not for ever anyway. No, us British, English – well, me – I'm not like them, I'm not flying the flag of revolution, I don't have fire in my belly or idealism on my tongue and I'm not singing the song of change and why? Because I don't know the words yet; but I will, we will. I won't be forgotten. **99**

The Pride

Alexi Kaye Campbell

☞ **WHO**   Sylvia, mid-thirties, middle class.

☞ **TO WHOM**   Oliver, mid-thirties, her close friend, gay.

☞ **WHERE**   A park bench, London.

☞ **WHEN**   2008.

☞ **WHAT HAS JUST HAPPENED**   The play tells the story of two sets of characters, both with the same names, from 1958 and from 2008. In 1958, Sylvia, is unhappily married to Philip. He is gay but in denial. When he meets her friend and colleague Oliver, he is unable to control his feelings of attraction. But the practice of homosexuality is illegal and their torrid affair ends unhappily. In 2008, Oliver and Philip, both friends of Sylvia's, are in a relationship and have been together for over a year. However, Oliver is promiscuous and Philip wants to end their relationship. They split up for a while but, with Sylvia's help, they will be reunited at Pride. Here, towards the end of the play and just before Philip arrives, Sylvia and Oliver are in the park where the Pride party is in full swing.

☞ **WHAT TO CONSIDER**

- Unlike her 1958 counterpart, Sylvia is confident, independent and happy.
- Sylvia is an actress and has just landed the role of Viola in *Twelfth Night* at Stratford.
- She has an Italian boyfriend called Mario and hopes one day to have children with him.
- She is very close to Oliver and has nursed him through difficult times.
- The punctuation. Notice how few full stops there are. What might this suggest about the rhythm and pace?
- Sylvia is impassioned, but try not to let the thoughts run away with you.

☞ **WHAT SHE WANTS**

- To express her disgust at the ignorance and narrow-mindedness of others.

- To protect Oliver from ridicule.

- For Oliver to take himself seriously. She fears he has become a caricature of himself.

- To shake him and to wake him up.

- To remind Oliver that his freedoms have been hard won.

- To politicise Oliver.

- To prepare Oliver for the necessary changes he must make in order to have a less selfish and more committed relationship with Philip.

☞ **KEYWORDS**   gay   shit   reduce   shallow   exile

Sylvia

66 And every second word is 'gay'. Gay this and gay that. 'You're so gay, it's so gay, they're so gay. Everything's gay.' So there's this one kid and she kind of looks a bit less scary than the rest of them and I just turn around and trying not to sound like her English teacher I say, 'Excuse me'… […] 'Excuse me, miss, but what exactly does that word mean? I mean, when you use it in that context. Like "That is such a gay song". When you say "That is such a gay song" what exactly does that mean?' […] She says it means 'shit'. It means it's shit. The word 'gay' is another word for saying 'shit'. […] I mean, the stuff you guys have to put up with. And then like literally the same evening I'm at Jennifer's for dinner. […] And she's invited another five or six people including some Spanish guy in pharmaceutics she's crazy about and Millie Wallis, who's had a massive nose job and looks completely different but nobody's allowed to talk about it so we're all pretending that even though her face is *entirely* different we haven't noticed a thing and there's this one guy who's being really quite annoying and pretending to be really liberal but saying something along the lines of, well, it kind of makes sense for the inheritance stuff but they don't really care about the other stuff, whatever that means, I mean, most of them just want to have fun and then Sonya's joining in and saying, and I quote, that 'some of her best friends are gay'... [...] But it's all kind of gone mad, she's saying, I mean, when's it going to stop and then she's going on about how most of the gay guys she knows are hedonists and spend most of their time in the gym and why should they want to imitate the straights anyway and it's all very much a chorus of 'we all love gay people and aren't they fun and if you ever need advice on wallpaper', but... [...] But I looked at them and they're all... [...] I suddenly looked at them and I was listening to what they were saying and they're not bad people, Oliver, I mean, a bit unimaginative, maybe, but not necessarily bad and I'm looking at them and I'm thinking... [...] Fuck, I don't know how to say this but they *reduce* you. [...] They reduce you, Oliver, to this person who is shallow. Someone who is defined by his body, by what he does with his body and by his taste in things. Clothes, interiors, whatever... [...] And the thing is you're so much more than that. And somewhere, *somewhere*, you, Oliver, have agreed with them. You've come to an agreement that this is what you are. [...] And I'm thinking of what it was that first made people question things, to push the boundaries, I mean, to stand up for themselves and to really fight and that what they were fighting for can't have been the right to fuck in parks and wear designer clothes... [...] After all, the only reason you were in the parks to begin with was because you couldn't be at home. You were kicked out, as it were. In exile. **99**

Push Up

Roland Schimmelpfennig, translated by Maja Zade

☞ **WHO**   Sabine, twenty-eight, Head of Department in a successful corporation.

☞ **TO WHOM**   The audience (see note on 'Direct audience address' in the introduction).

☞ **WHERE**   A top executive's office.

☞ **WHEN**   Present day.

☞ **WHAT HAS JUST HAPPENED**   The speech that follows comes close to the start of the play. It interrupts a scene between Sabine and Angelika, a top executive and wife of Sabine's boss, Kramer. Sabine has requested this meeting with Angelika to find out why she has turned Sabine down for the Delhi job. It is the job that everyone wants and one for which Sabine feels more than qualified. Read the play to find out what happens next.

☞ **WHAT TO CONSIDER**

- The style of the play. Scenes are interrupted while characters talk directly to the audience.
- The language. Sentences are short and to the point.
- Sabine is competitive and ambitious. We know from Angelika that she has 'climbed the ladder fast here'. Note how she describes her colleagues as 'average' or 'very average'.
- Status is important to her.
- Her wardrobe is an outward manifestation of her position in the hierarchy, but it is also problematic for her. On the surface, she appears in control, but the trauma she experiences getting dressed in the morning shows her neurosis.
- Angelika has a similar struggle and delivers a speech that, in places, echoes Sabine's almost word for word. Power-dressing is an important part of this corporate world.

☞ **WHAT SHE WANTS**

- To reveal the truth about herself. Note how different she is in this direct address to the audience compared to the way she is with Angelika.

- To explain the monotony and loneliness of her life. For all her success, she feels left out. It pains her to think that she has gone without sex for two whole years when she is in her prime. She longs for intimacy.

☞ **KEYWORDS**   cold   nothing   problem   ordeal   difficult   dark   awful   ugly   impossible   terrible

Sabine

❝ I haven't had sex in two years. And I'm twenty-eight. I get up at six every morning. I take a cold shower and then I have breakfast. Usually fruit. In my dressing gown. While I watch TV. I do that every morning except Sunday. In the morning I watch TV from half past six until seven. The programme's not very good at that time but I sit in front of the TV and think about nothing.

Then I start to get dressed. I never wear the same thing as the day before. Never. Although my clothes often look similar. I have many clothes. Heaps. I chose my apartment with this in mind. Built-in cupboards. In my current flat there are two built-in cupboards.

I can't decide what to wear. It's a problem. I often change my clothes completely several times over before I can decide what to wear. Until I've managed to make a decision. It's not easy. It's an ordeal.

When I'm dressed I blow-dry my hair and put on make-up. My hairstyle is okay, there's not much you can do with my hair. Make-up is difficult, especially in winter, when it's still dark outside. Not too much. Just high-quality products. From Japan for example.

Short pause.

When I've done my face I take the lift to the basement garage. It's eight o'clock now. Halfway down I stop and turn back. Go back up. Because I feel awful. I can't stand it. I can't stand it. I unlock the two safety locks to my apartment and get changed. I don't like what I'm wearing. I usually wear blue. I don't really like blue except maybe jeans or winter sweaters, but nonetheless I usually wear blue. I've taken to wearing everything in blue. To buy blue clothes when I have the time. Everything I buy is blue. So – everything's colour coordinated.

Nonetheless I turn around halfway down and get changed again. I change everything. My stockings, my knickers, my bra. I feel ugly. I have to hurry, the clock's ticking, and I'm standing in front of the mirror in the hall feeling ugly.

After a while it's gone half past eight. It's time, I need to go. Again I take the lift to the basement garage. Get into the car. I can't turn back now. To turn back now is completely impossible. I look in the rear-view mirror. My make-up is terrible. I don't like my lipstick. In the traffic jam on the circular I redo my lips. I can't do my eyes until I'm in the office. Whatever you do, don't look cheap.

I arrive at the office and I feel like no one's looking at me. That's good. That's awful.

At nine fifteen I see my team. None of the women at the long table wear blue. Except for when they wear jeans or winter sweaters maybe, but you don't see a lot of those here. In the meetings. Many of them are average. Very average. Most of them.

None of them wear blue.

Short pause.

I look into the faces at the table and I ask myself which of them had sex last night, and how often. Or this morning. While I took a cold shower. While I watched TV and thought about nothing.

All of them, I think. All of them except me. **„**

Rabbit

Nina Raine

☞ **WHO**   Bella, twenty-nine, middle class, works in PR.

☞ **TO WHOM**   Her friends Emily and Sandy, and her ex-lovers Richard and Tom.

☞ **WHERE**   The restaurant of a private members' club, London.

☞ **WHEN**   Present day (although strictly speaking before the public smoking ban of 2007).

☞ **WHAT HAS JUST HAPPENED**   Bella is celebrating her twenty-ninth birthday with her two girlfriends Emily and Sandy, her ex-boyfriend Richard and ex-lover Tom, whom she has met by chance in the bar that night. Their conversation centres around matters of sex and the differences between male and female attitudes. Richard, Sandy and Bella are combative, and as they all become increasingly drunk the exchanges become more heated. Meanwhile, Bella's father is in hospital suffering with a brain tumour. He is dying. Flashback scenes of his relationship with Bella as a child, teenager and adult intercut the main action. Then, when Richard poses the question, 'Who thinks they'll get married?', it starts a debate about love, romance and sexual jealousy. Bella was unfaithful to Richard in their relationship. She slept with Tom while she was still with Richard, and during the course of the evening Richard and Tom make this connection. Richard accuses Bella of never trying to see things from anyone else's perspective. He asks her, 'Why don't you care any more?' The speech that follows is made up of her response to him.

☞ **WHAT TO CONSIDER**

- Bella's inner turmoil. She knows deep down she should be with her father in hospital and not out celebrating with friends.

- Her relationship with her father. She says they don't get on. This is not the full story. Read the play to understand its complexity.

- Bella dropped out of a law course because she felt she was not clever enough. She now works for a PR company which

she describes as 'a stupid, mindless, waste-of-time job'. She
earns a lot of money.

- Richard is a barrister. He and Bella were together on and off
  for five years. Richard wanted to marry her.

- Tom works in the city. Theirs was a relationship based on
  sexual attraction. Bella tells Emily that apart from having a
  good time in bed, she and Tom had nothing in common.

- The stress of being twenty-nine, one year off thirty, when one
  is supposed to have become an adult and have everything
  sorted. And when there is no going back!

☞ **WHAT SHE WANTS**

- To defend/fight her corner and to explain herself. Note how,
  halfway through the speech, she says, 'I did see it from your
  perspective, Richard.'

- To apologise for her bad behaviour.

- To ensure she does not end up like her mother.

☞ **KEYWORDS**   (*note how many of them are to do with a
judgement of some kind*) right   wrong   good   important
clever   tougher   harder   better   shit   ruined   lost   wasting

Bella

❝ Richard, you don't really know my father. [...] Do you
know *why* my father always thinks he's right? And that I'm
wrong? [...] Because I'm a woman and he's a man. Deep
down, privately, he doesn't think women are as good as men.
Nearly as good, but not quite.

That's why he reminds me of you.

So my mother will *never* be as important as him...

And my father thinks – he loves me very much, he loves us all
very much – but deep down he thinks – my brothers are the
talented ones. The clever ones.

They're the ones he's proud of.

Not me. [...] It is true.

Beat.

And it makes me feel competitive. Angry and competitive. I think, you're wrong. That's my reaction. You're wrong and I'm going to prove you wrong. I'll be tougher, and harder, and better. Because I'm right. Women can be better.

(*To* RICHARD.) I did see it from your perspective, Richard.

I felt what you felt. Jealousy.

But I think it comes with love. And I decided not to be in love. I didn't want to feel it. I decided to be hard.

Like you said.

And I know I ruined it.

And I'm sorry.

Beat.

I felt it with you. [*i.e. with* TOM]

Beat.

And it felt – it didn't feel like I thought it would.

Because it felt – more than anything else, in the end, it felt – competitive.

Competitive and angry.

I thought, you're not going to treat me like shit. I'm going to treat you like shit. First.

I ruined it when I tried not to care. And I ruined it when I did. [...] And I lost.

(*To* RICHARD.) And you think that makes me into a person who doesn't believe in love. You think I've decided to be a selfish, domineering, hard person.

And I think you're a selfish, domineering, sentimental person.

I annoy you. And you annoy me.

But you're right. I am deliberately hard, domineering, and selfish. And you know why? Because I saw my mother wasting her whole life on other people. Mainly my father. And I don't want to do that. **"**

random

debbie tucker green

☞ **WHO**   Sister, young black woman from South London.

☞ **TO WHOM**   The audience (see note on 'Direct audience address' in the introduction).

☞ **WHERE**   Unspecified, but could be played as it is described, i.e. the hospital/mortuary, the police car, the murder spot. South London.

☞ **WHEN**   Present day.

☞ **WHAT HAS JUST HAPPENED**   It is an ordinary day much like any other in the lives of an Afro-Caribbean family. The father is asleep after working the night shift, the mother goes shopping for food, the sister goes to work, and the brother goes to school. But at 1.30 p.m. the brother is fatally wounded, stabbed on the high street in his lunch hour. The police go to the house where they inform the mother and father. The mother texts her daughter: 'Come home. Now.' The sister returns. Then she and her father go to identify the body.

☞ **WHAT TO CONSIDER**

- All parts are played by the same black actress.

- Although the speech starts in the past tense, it quickly moves to the present. You might want to imagine that you are in the morgue, then the police car and then finally at the scene of the crime as if the events were happening now.

- She is in shock, but articulate. The language is heightened, poetic. There are many key words, giving weight and meaning. Connect to them.

☞ **WHAT SHE WANTS**

- To give support to her father.

- To see with her own eyes what they have done to her brother.

- To describe in acute detail what it is she sees. Note how she describes the cut that kills him. It is as tiny as the moment of senselessness. To what extent does the realisation that he was stabbed in the back 'those rules is broken then – ' enrage her?

☞ **KEYWORDS**   chunk   horrific   slashed   mark   kill/killer cut   broken   gash   deep   hole   heavy   silence   murder battlefield   slain

Sister

❝ Dad went down to ID my brother.
I went down to support our dad.

Dad went in
I didn't have to follow.
But…

Brother had a –
birthmark.
Here.
Juss like me.
But his been
cut thru
with a chunk of him gone
now.
He had an eye
two.
Now he got juss one.
They try to pretty it up
mek it look like he winkin…
But
… you can't pretty up
whass horrific.
Y'not meant to.

His mout'
look like a clown –
now

wider than it should be.
It slashed so much on a one side
from there
to there.

That juss he's face.
Thass juss the ones that would mark him,
wouldn't kill him.

Apparently.

Thass juss the ones he'd haveta live with.
Have had to live with.

He have plenty little
like – uh – like –
(*gestures forearms*)
look like he a self-harmer
but proof he fought back.
Then they have to turn him
and
hold him
an'
lie him on his side
an'
so we could see – could see good
lookin hard to see.

Point of entry.
The killer cut.

You have to look hard
to look hard.

This was…
the smallest.
The cleanest.
The easiest to miss
part of it all.
Truss mi.
Juss –
round.
(*gestures*)
From the back –

those rules is broken then –
thru to –
(*gestures*)
punctured his...
su'un – important.
But.
Not no gash.
Not no not sure.
Not no random.
Juss a small
deep
sorta
round
sorta
hole.
In him.

Easy to miss.
Easy to miss.

Easy to miss.

(*Beat.*)

And our dad the kinda dad who...
Who...
don't say nuthin –
unless he –
who won't say anythin –
unless...
Dad tryin to say somethin.
Dad's tryin to say somethin
but
... nu'un won't [come out]...

I watch.
Watch him.
... He's embarrassed.
I watch his embarrassment.
I can't look away.

Where do it say –
this is part of it?

They lift us back
in a unmarked ride,
tho I can still tell iss one of theirs.
And me an' Dad sit
in the back –
like kids
as they drive us home
havin to ask directions.
The only thing breakin the heavy silence.

And I still ent stopped
starin at Dad.
Dad still ent stopped
lookin away
and we pass the everyday
the life goes on
the
people goin about they business
the
people who don't know – won't know – don't got no idea.

We pass the spot.
I ask –
to stop. Get let out and get out.
As they drive on.

Standin by the yellow an' blue murder board
the battlefield where brother slain.
Alone.
Me on my own.
Cept for the boys in blue
guarding the pavement piece
I guess.
Watchin
the Police tape bouncing
in the breeze.
Too late. **99**

Scenes from the Big Picture
Owen McCafferty

☞ **WHO**   Maeve Hynes, late twenties, Northern Irish.

☞ **TO WHOM**   Joe Hynes, her husband.

☞ **WHERE**   Downstairs in their house in an imagined area of
Belfast. The exact room is not specified. It could be in the hallway,
kitchen or sitting room. You decide.

☞ **WHEN**   Present day, summer.

☞ **WHAT HAS JUST HAPPENED**   The play follows a day in the
life of twenty-one characters whose stories are interwoven.
Maeve and Joe Hynes have been together for ten years, but are
having trouble conceiving a child. Maeve is becoming increasingly
anxious and Joe has started an affair with Helen Woods, a
barmaid who works in a local pub. Maeve has spent the day
comforting and supporting her cousin, who gave birth to a little
boy. Joe, who has been promoted to shop steward in an abattoir,
has had a day of increasing stress. The business is on the verge
of collapse, and he has been required to make some difficult
decisions. Amidst all this he has been calling Helen on his mobile
phone. It is a small community, and at one point Helen was in
the same shop as Maeve, who was buying baby cream. Joe also
made time to visit Helen at the pub where they had oral sex.
Meanwhile, at the hospital with her cousin, Maeve stole a
dummy baby that they give to mothers-to-be to practise on.
When Joe arrives home he thinks it is a real baby and that she
has snatched it out of desperation. He threatens to report her
and, while he considers her to be in such a crazed state, uses the
opportunity to reveal his true feelings towards her and about
their marriage. He lets slip that he would rather be somewhere
else. When Maeve shows him that the baby is a dummy, it is too
late for him to go back on what he has said. The truth is out, and
Maeve realises that he no longer wants to be with her. Her
speech is in response to Joe saying, 'a didn't mean things to
happen this way'.

☞ **WHAT TO CONSIDER**

- The speech comes at the end of a long, hot day. Both Maeve and Joe are at breaking point.

- He loved her once. To what extent does she still love him? Note how amidst all the pain and hurt she offers to iron his clothes. What does it tell you about the marriage? Is it an indication that she still loves him enough to prevent him from going about in creased clothing or is it just that old habits die hard? Is it to do with her pride? Whatever you decide, it is a touching and poignant detail.

- The moment of realisation – 'i know who it is'. Don't rush this. Read the whole play so you know what incident Maeve is recalling. You may like to imagine 'Helen' as someone you know who is prettier/younger/more overtly sexual than you consider yourself to be in order for you to connect to Maeve's feelings of hurt and humiliation.

- The language and punctuation. Note how the playwright uses only lower-case letters. There are no commas or full stops, only dashes where a character might take a breath and have a change of thought. What does this suggest to you? How might this determine the playing of the speech in terms of rhythm and pace?

☞ **WHAT SHE WANTS**

- To assert herself.

- To ascertain who or what Joe means when he tells her, 'a want to be somewhere else'.

- To extricate herself from the pain the marriage has brought.

- To, as she puts it herself, 'maintain what little dignity I have left'.

- To express her hurt and anger and for Joe to hear it.

☞ **KEYWORDS** pretending pocket fault guilty forgive wrong fuck justify hurt lighter dignity cut

Maeve

❝ what way did ya mean them to happen – that i would never know and you could go on pretending – or maybe i was to find somethin in yer pocket – somethin to give the game away and i was to confront ya – and somehow it would all turn round that it's my fault – and although i wasn't happy with the situation i would feel a bit guilty about it all – so i would forgive you – and we could go through the rest of our lives me thinking what's wrong with me – what is it about me that makes my husband want to fuck other women – and you thinkin these things happen – that's the way of the world – is that the way ya meant it to happen – jesus – a thought just came to me there – i know who it is – a don't know her but a saw her – kept lookin at me that whole time i was in the shop – this girl kept lookin at me then if i caught her eye she'd look away – she runs the pub or somethin – it's her isn't it […] doesn't matter – it is though i know it is […] don't say a damn thing – i'm not givin ya the chance to justify yerself that's not goin to happen – you hurt me joe an that's it – that's all ya need to understand – funny thing i feel in some way – lighter – when a was up at the hospital today lookin at all those babies i kept thinkin maybe joe an i aren't right for havin children – that was the first time a thought that – i think that's why a brought the doll home – to give us a chance to prove me wrong – ya can take one of the good suitcases – i'll iron some clothes for you […] ya don't have a choice joe – i'm doin my best to maintain what little dignity i have left – if you were to stay here joe i'd only end up havin to cut yer fuckin eyes out – a wouldn't be pretendin either **❞**

Strawberries in January

Evelyne de la Chenelière, in a version by Rona Munro

☞ **WHO**   Sophie, twenty-eight. (The play was originally written in Quebec French. This version is written with Scottish characters in mind, but works well in any accent.)

☞ **TO WHOM**   Francois.

☞ **WHERE**   Francois's café, Montreal.

☞ **WHEN**   Present day.

☞ **WHAT HAS JUST HAPPENED**   The speech that follows comes close to the start of the play. Robert, a university lecturer, has come into the café where he knows Francois works. They met for the first time some nights earlier, got quite drunk, and Francois (a would-be writer) had started to tell Robert about his relationship with a woman called Sophie. It is early in the morning some days later, and Robert, intrigued by the story, has come unexpectedly into the café to find Francois. Robert wants to hear how the story ends. As Francois continues, the actress playing Sophie enters and her 'story' is told in the form of a flashback sequence. Here she is on her way to work, but has stopped off at the café with a punnet of out-of-season (it is January) strawberries for him. She has something she wants to say.

☞ **WHAT TO CONSIDER**

- The play follows the fortunes of four 'romantically challenged singletons'. It is funny and touching and has a happy ending.

- The play goes backwards and forwards in time, characters talk to the audience, and there is a playfulness about the style and tone.

- The punctuation. There are very few commas and full stops in the speech. Watch that, in the playing of it, your thoughts do not run away with you.

- Sophie has a lust for life, what the French would describe as a *'joie de vivre'*.

- She is a romantic. Her gift of the strawberries in January is a lovely example of this. (In a later scene Francois tells her he loves her, but they are in the launderette and Sophie is unimpressed.)

☞ WHAT SHE WANTS

- Romance.
- Experiences that are out of the ordinary.
- To explain and to justify her forwardness.
- To convince Francois that marriage is the best and most obvious step.
- For Francois to say 'Yes.'

☞ KEYWORDS   supposed   agony   separate   tear   grab together   conventionally/conventional   unconventional

Sophie

❝ I know this isn't the way you're supposed to do it and that is a bit of a worry but I said to myself life's short and if everyone always waits for everyone else to make the first move you can waste an awful lot of time and I know you sometimes watch me sleeping I know because I'm not actually sleeping and you can't deny it, yesterday for instance you were watching me sleeping and I know when we're drinking wine and talking in the sitting room together until two in the morning it's just agony for both of us to go to our separate beds and even if every couple tears each other apart and we've both made fun of all those couples that tear each other apart I think we owe it to ourselves to try and grab something that might tear us apart. And I don't see why if we like shopping together, doing the housework together, eating breakfast together, watching old films together, I don't really see why we wouldn't like making love together, because that's something a lot more exciting, it seems to me, than shopping, housework, and old films so I'm asking you to marry me in the spring. I know, conventionally I'm not supposed to be the one who asks but you prefer the unconventional so I'm asking you to marry me in the spring. Or outside, next winter, because it's conventional to get married in spring. [...] That was the moment when you would have kissed me or something so I don't really know what to say now. [...] I tried this out in front of the mirror this morning to see how it came over and I thought I was quite moving? [...] I suppose we can talk about it tonight. 🟥

Terminus
Mark O'Rowe

☞ **WHO**   'B' – Female, twenties, from Dublin.

☞ **TO WHOM**   The audience (see note on 'Direct audience address' in the introduction).

☞ **WHERE**   Unspecified. You may prefer to imagine you are in all the different locations as she describes them.

☞ **WHEN**   Present day. After dark.

☞ **WHAT HAS JUST HAPPENED**   The play is a series of three interconnected monologues charting the events of one extraordinary night in and around Dublin. The speech that follows forms the start of character B's story.

☞ **WHAT TO CONSIDER**

- The play is fantastical. What starts out as an ordinary evening for B, soon becomes a trip of supernatural proportions. Read the play to find out what happens when she falls from a crane but is saved from instant death by a flying demon whose face is composed of worms.

- The language. Poetic and muscular, the text is as heightened as its subject matter. You can be bold in your playing of it.

- The use of rhyming words throughout the speech. Make space for these words to land. They are like the beat of music and should pulse through you, driving you on.

- Her backstory. Later on in the play, as she contemplates death, she is besieged by memories. They reveal much about her character and troubled personality and go some way to explaining why trust is such an important issue for her:

  She had a baby sister who died after only an hour and forty minutes.

  Her father died of lung cancer.

  Her mother had an affair with B's boyfriend. When B found out, she attempted suicide. The relationship between mother and daughter remains fraught.

- Her name. The playwright has purposefully omitted to supply this detail. What might this suggest?

☞ WHAT SHE WANTS

- To escape her loneliness.
- To protect herself from hurt and at the same time to be able to trust someone again.
- To find love, to love and be loved.

☞ KEYWORDS   (*there are many*) sink adieu depart
identical reflex illusion aborting self-isolation
forbearance endurance

☞ NB   This play offers a number of other speeches from which to choose.

B

❝ Every night at five… […] I leave work… […] and meander the minute or so to McGurk's; sink one, sink two, then bid adieu to the barman – his reply to me each and every time, 'God bless' – depart then, head to the M&S, my dinner to purchase, my day-to-day to adhere to, near to identical all, said days, near rote, you know? Near reflex now.

The bus home then, the silent flat. No cat nor any kind of pet. The sofa – sit. The telly – hit the remote. Reward – the illusion of presence through voices.

Unpack my choices of purchase. Wine: pour, then sip it. My meal: unseal, then flip it into the microwave: shepherd's pie, my favourite dish. Now, why on earth would I think that mattered?

Shattered as shit tonight, I sit, sort through some bills. The telephone trills, my wine spills on my lap. I curse, say, 'Fuck,' pick up.

'Hello?'

'Hello!'

It's Lee, who wants to know if I'd like to go for a drink with herself and Lenny, her loving hubby.

I refuse politely. Lonely as I might be, as I am, I can't abide or suffer the fucker, his swagger, his subtle suggestions; insinuations intimating coupling, couple of times a touch in passing – my behind, my back – Lee's lack of acknowledgement disappointing. But, what's worse is that his vying for me's not just fun. He's overcome when I'm around with a want that's potent and profound, which, bound together with his sleaziness, causes me a great deal of unease, I guess.

My shepherd's pie beeps and I take it, make to unwrap it. The covering jams so I jerk and unjam it with too much force, so it flips and falls – face first, I predict, and am proved correct – the plummet's conclusion a meeting of meat and floor, in effect, aborting my dinner.

I stare at the mess a moment, unmoving, the checking of tears proving fruitless. Doubtless a symptom of self-isolation, the crushing frustration that ushers one night to the next. Tonight more pronounced, the attack unannounced; my reaction surprising me equally. 'Fuck it,' I utter, and phone Lee back, tell her I've changed my mind in fact.

She says, 'Great. How's nine?' An hour. Enough time to shower and so forth, check before I go forth, for keys. Pockets. I can't leave without them. Empty. Now, where the hell did I put them? The kitchen, the counter, swipe them, stop. The slop. I won't bother cleaning it up.

The bus, the seat behind the driver; tactics for the immediate future: forebearance, endurance, tolerate Lenny; have patience when he tries to harass me.

He doesn't, surprisingly. Half an hour there, or here, so far, he's behaving. We're drinking beer, Lee raving on about saving, the fact that she can't, when her rant is cut short by this dude exhuding sex appeal, who steals a look in passing, stops and curses, 'Fuck!' reverses, and, of course, is a friend of Lenny and Lee's.

'Jesus, what are the chances?' he says, and glances at me with a smile to be filed under, 'Most attractive I've seen in a while'. 〟

This Wide Night

Chloë Moss

☞ **WHO**   Marie, thirty, working class.

☞ **TO WHOM**   Lorraine, fifty.

☞ **WHERE**   Marie's bedsit, London.

☞ **WHEN**   Present day.

☞ **WHAT HAS JUST HAPPENED**   At the start of the play,
Lorraine arrives unexpectedly at Marie's bedsit. She has just been
released from prison where (until Marie's earlier release) she and
Marie were cellmates. Marie is surprised to see her. Lorraine is on
her way to the hostel where she has been found a place to stay.
She is hungry and thirsty, so Marie gets a pizza for them. Lorraine
is clearly frightened, and Marie suggests she stays the night. Marie
then tells Lorraine she has got a late shift and has to go to work.
When Marie returns to the bedsit at 2.30 a.m. the next morning,
she wakes Lorraine. Sharing Marie's bed they both then try to
sleep but are overtired. It is raining hard, and Marie is reminded
of her first night in prison with Lorraine: 'I thought you was a
nutter at first… Goin' on about meditating to the sound of the
fuckin' rain.' Then Marie tells Lorraine about the 'game' she used
to play with herself when she was little and, by the end of the
speech that follows, Lorraine is fast asleep.

☞ **WHAT TO CONSIDER**

- The play takes its inspiration from real-life events and was first
  produced by Clean Break theatre company, who work with
  women whose lives have been affected by the criminal justice
  system.
- Strictly speaking they are lying in bed and Lorraine is stroking
  Marie's hair. However, for the purposes of an audition, you may
  wish to restage the scene with Marie sitting up in bed or
  sitting on a chair. You decide.
- Marie was a drug addict when she arrived in prison. Apart
  from smoking and drinking, she is now clean.

- Her ex-boyfriend is a violent drug addict. He wants Marie back. Marie tells Lorraine that she won't take him back unless he can change.

- She has told Lorraine that she works at The Windmill pub on Brixton Lane.

- Later on in the play we discover that Marie has lied to Lorraine about her boyfriend and her job at the pub.

- The immense difficulty of leaving prison and resettling into a life on the outside.

- Throughout the play the women struggle to redefine their relationship in its new context.

☞ **WHAT SHE WANTS**

- To comfort and to reassure herself.

- To surrender in this moment to the same feeling of closeness she had with Lorraine in prison.

☞ **KEYWORDS**   alright   nice   rich   poor   herpes

Marie

❝ I used to do this thing when I was little. Raindrop racing. I'd fix on two drops. One would be me and the other one would be any kid in school who was doing alright, like if they had a nice mum and dad or a nice house.

Mostly it was Charlotte Hughes coz her mum worked in Greggs and put cream cakes in her packed lunch.

Sometimes my one'd stop and hang on another raindrop and I'd imagine that was when I went to stay with Auntie Barbara or Mr and Mrs Dent or Sam and Jason's then it'd separate and roll down and catch up with Charlotte Hughes.

Aim of the game was that if you got down first then you'd be alright.

Auntie Barbara, she weren't my proper auntie but she made me call her that for some reason, she used to say, 'Not everyone can be alright, Marie. The world isn't like that. Some people are rich and some people are poor and some people's mothers work in Greggs and some don't. Not everyone can be alright. That isn't how things work.'

I didn't have anything against Charlotte Hughes.

She used to break off bits of cake when I asked for a bit. But I weren't allowed to take a bite. She'd go, 'You've always got cold sores, Marie, and once you catch one you've got herpes for life.'

So I used to have me nose pressed against the window willing myself to stop hanging about and get down to the finish line.

Charlotte's raindrop usually zig-zagged along no sweat but if she did brush against another one I reckoned it'd be something nice like popping into a friend's for tea then she'd be on her way, holding one of them party bags with flumps and fruit-salad chews in it.

Once, David Harper was the other raindrop because he had a nan who knitted clothes for his action men.

Beat.

I still do it now sometimes. That game.

Silence. LORRAINE *has started to snore quietly.*

Lorraine? (*Beat.*) Lol. **"**

What We Know

Pamela Carter

☞ **WHO**   Lucy, thirties, Scottish.

☞ **TO WHOM**   Helen, an emergency-call handler, Charlie, a neighbour and Cal, Lucy's college friend.

☞ **WHERE**   Lucy's kitchen.

☞ **WHEN**   Present day.

☞ **WHAT HAS JUST HAPPENED**   Lucy and her partner Jo have invited friends over and are preparing a meal together. As they are cooking, Jo, 'as if by magic', disappears into nowhere, and moments later a teenage boy appears out of the blue. Lucy has never met the boy. He helps her prepare a table for a dinner party and then leaves. No sooner as he does so Helen arrives followed by Charlie and then Cal. What started out as an ordinary evening soon takes a surreal turn as Lucy is forced to recall Jo's death. The 'nine minutes' referred to in the speech that follows is the time it took for the ambulance to arrive.

☞ **WHAT TO CONSIDER**

- Jo's death was sudden and completely unexpected.
- Before he died they were discussing their future.
- The play reminds us of just how fragile our lives can be.
- Note how the playwright has chosen to write solely in lower case.

☞ **WHAT SHE WANTS**

- To come to terms with what has happened.
- Reassurance that she did the right thing.
- To give voice to her feelings of abject sadness and emptiness.

☞ **KEYWORDS**   babbling   dying   leaving   swore   obtuse clear   pure   straight   dead   sadness   heavy   emptied   hole strange   massive

Lucy

❝ nine minutes. and he was still mine. tell me, helen. what happened? [...] those nine minutes. you stayed on the phone, didn't you? you asked me things. you told me what to do. [...] you asked me if he was agitated or aggressive. you asked me if i thought he could understand me, if he could speak. yes? [...] you said i should see if he could squeeze my hand. [...] you asked me if i thought he was finding it hard to breathe. you said to look at the colour of his lips.

and you told me to keep talking to him. 'talk to jo; he can hear you.' even though he couldn't move or speak.

and i did? [...] nine minutes. i had his hand. i held his hand. i said... what?

i can see his hand in mine. and i can feel us. and my lips are moving but i can't hear the words. i'm babbling. saying nothing. saying everything's going to be just fine.

you told me to keep talking to him because your hearing is the last thing to go, isn't it? when you're dying?

HELEN *nods.*

yes, i knew that. i'd heard that before somewhere. that's why i kept talking. because he was leaving me.

i swore at him. [...] i wanted to be good and say the best for us both. tell him what he needed to hear. i wanted to explain myself.

i said i was sorry for being obtuse, for being difficult. i never meant to be. i don't mean to be. i want to be clear and pure and straight.

i should've said more. i wish i'd... i tried... this is really fucking hard.

i said 'jo, listen. listen to this.' i said 'jo, i've kept what you've told me. it's here. always.

i know only ever to use the freshest eggs for poaching. i know that hot milk makes your mashed potato fluffy. i know that a warm bowl makes for a better sponge.

i know that i've been loved. i know what you know. please know how much i love you.'

that's it. god, is that it? […] jo is dead. you asked me how i am. well, i can tell you. i can tell you how i feel, cal. […] i feel full of sadness. full of it. heavy with it. and at the same time, i feel like i've been emptied out. dug out like a big hole.

isn't that strange? isn't it strange that jo's not being here is so big, so massive, that it is here? it's absolutely this. now.

there. this probably wasn't the kind of evening you were hoping for. […] it's okay. it's fine, isn't it? all fine. because here we are safe and well. and on we go.

has everyone finished?

they nod.

then i'll clear this away. […] if you want to go, then please… there's really not much to hang around for. […] i did make a pudding. […] but i doubt it's any good. **99**